Jennifer Elizabeth Plunk.

Building Successful
Training Programs

Building Successful Training Programs

A Step-by-Step Guide

Kay Tytler Abella

Addison-Wesley Publishing Company, Inc.
Reading, Massachusetts • Menlo Park, California
Don Mills, Ontario • Wokingham, England
Amsterdam • Sydney • Singapore • Tokyo
Mexico City • Bogotá • Santiago • San Juan

LIBRARY OF CONGRESS CATALOGING-IN-PUBLICATION DATA

Abella, Kay Tytler.
  Building successful training programs.

  Includes index.
  1. Employees, Training of. I. Title.
HF5549.5.T7A26   1986   658.3'12404   85-15714
ISBN 0-201-00100-4

Cover design by Marshall Henrichs
Text design by Joyce C. Weston
Set in 11-point sabon by Compset, Beverly, MA

  BCDEFGHIJ-AL-89876

Second Printing, November 1986

For my husband,
Luis

CONTENTS

Part Three
Glossary and Index   141

INTRODUCTION

Training programs are a lot like theatre. In the blush of a successful opening night, there is a sense of exhilaration and relief that "they liked it!" Designers, developers, and writers all sit in the back row of the classroom, holding their breath until the final curtain, waiting to see if the reviews will be raves.

It is exciting when you have a hit; it is often excruciating when you have a flop.

But the development of a training program does not need to be a hit-or-miss, "try it one more time" experience. There is a logical and comprehensive series of actions that will dramatically increase your chances of a "hit" and help you get it right the first time around.

It has been my frustrating experience to see people spend far more time, money, and energy than necessary putting together a training program — and sometimes never getting it right — because they leave out steps, shorten the process, or carry out the steps haphazardly.

I've seen a creative design that could not do its job because it was build on perceived needs which the attendees never had. I've seen a design that was right on target end up as a meaningless program because no one ever looked at whether the materials did what the design intended. I've seen a program rich in content fall on its face because the flow of topics was confusing and choppy. I've seen a beautifully constructed exercise rendered useless by a failure to test whether instructions were clear.

Why?

Sometimes people just don't know how to perform the steps

needed to create a successful program. Sometimes the pressure of time and resources makes people shorten the process. Yet they don't understand the function of each step clearly enough to head off the resulting problems. Sometimes people just let things drift because they don't have a disciplined process to keep them on track during the design and development stages.

Whatever the reason, the result is the same — a training program that is at best irrelevant or uninteresting and at worst brings on talk of beheading the training professional.

Excellence is a great topic of discussion in organizations today. Excellence in training programs is the result of a dash of inspiration up front and a lot of organization, thoroughness, and attention to details in bringing the inspiration to its final form.

This book describes a process that will provide the discipline and guidance to bring your training program to "opening night" with confidence, efficiency, and outstanding results.

HOW TO USE THIS BOOK

This book is designed to be a practical guide to the design and development of training programs, from the original definition of the training needs through the pilot session of the program. It also examines the major training methodologies and how to use them effectively. The way you use the book depends on how you are involved with training.

If you have just gotten into training, either full time or as part of your job, you can use the book to see what training is about and as a reference book in the ways described below.

If you are a line manager involved in a training project, the book will help you understand what training professionals will need from you and why.

If you are already a training professional in an organization or a training consultant you may use this book in the following ways:

- to work through each step in detail, as a program is being developed
- to refer quickly to a single point or step when a question arises
- to define who is going to do what when a number of people are working on the same program

- to explain to outside consultants the process you want to use with them
- to explain to program sponsors or other line managers the process that will be used to develop a program and the support that will be needed from them
- to analyze why the development process has not worked properly for a given program and to determine what actions are needed to remedy the situation
- to make sure the standard process used by your training organization is complete and consistent
- to train a new member of your training organization

THE DESIGN AND DEVELOPMENT PROCESS

The ten steps in the design and development process are:

Step 1. Gathering Information on Training Needs

Step 2. Preparing the Program Specifications Document

Step 3. Conducting the Design Meeting

Step 4. Preparing the Design Document

Step 5. Preparing the Materials List and Project Plan

Step 6. Gathering Information for Program Materials

Step 7. Writing Materials

Step 8. Reviewing Materials Against the Design Document

Step 9. Conducting the Materials Test

Step 10. Holding the Pilot Program

The chapter describing each step includes the following:

- Definition: what you need to do during the step
- Importance: why it is important to include the step
- Execution: exactly how to carry out the step, including — where needed — samples, agendas, content descriptions, and how to handle common obstacles
- Requirements: the materials, time, people, budget, and facilities you will need for the step

- Line Review: for those steps requiring line review (steps 2, 4, and 8), what is involved in the review.
- Remember: the key points to keep in mind as you work through the step
- Looking Ahead: how the step links to the next one in the process

The final chapter in Part One describes how to analyze and fix a program that is not working.

Part Two of the book describes the major training program techniques and methodologies available to program designers, such as case studies, role-plays, task forces, individual exercises, and group discussions. Each methodology is described in terms of when and how it is used, how to develop the needed materials, and common pitfalls in developing materials to use with the methodology. One chapter presents some guidelines for exercise instructions. The final chapter describes the special requirements of using video technology in training programs.

Following an organized process is an excellent way to ensure that all the critical steps are carried out. I have, therefore, presented the process in its ideal form, recognizing that limited time and resources will not always allow you to follow it exactly. Accordingly, in the chapter on each step, I have suggested possible short cuts as well as the obstacles inherent in them.

ASSUMPTIONS

This model will be helpful in the design and development of most training experiences. However, as described in this book it applies primarily to training programs that have certain characteristics.

First of all, I assume that the program being developed concerns analytic or interactive skills or knowledge not technical skills. While the basics of the process will apply to the development of any training experience, some adaptations may be necessary if you are teaching a technical skill, such as welding or CPR.

At the same time, I assume that the training to be designed has a practical focus and will be interactive and participative. Most of my examples concern classroom programs for groups of twenty-five or under, using primarily written or audiovisual materials.

I also assume that the organization that is developing the training program wants to use currently accepted principles of adult learning, such as relevancy, use of participants' experience, planning for application of new knowledge, and opportunities to practice, with feedback to participants. These principles are outlined in more detail in Step 3 on the design meeting.

I use the terms *program sponsor, project manager,* and *design team* to cover a number of situations. Program sponsor refers to that person or persons who requested the program. The project manager is the person who is primarily responsible for developing the program. He or she actually does most of the design and development work or is responsible for putting together a team to do the necessary tasks. Design team describes the group of people involved in the design and development of the program. Sometimes the "team" will be a single person; other times, a large number of people.

If the program development is being done entirely within the organization that will be using it, then the program sponsor is probably a line manager. He or she could also be a regional or divisional human resources person. The project manager may be a member of the training department. If the training department is developing the program as part of the general training function, then the project manager could be the program sponsor as well.

If you are an independent consultant delivering training services to a particular organization, then your program sponsor is your client, whether that person is someone from the organization's training department or a line manager. If you are developing a program for a general market, then you yourself are both the program sponsor and the project manager.

ACKNOWLEDGMENTS

We all know how hard it is to identify the role a training experience may have played in a person's ultimate job success. It is equally difficult to untangle the many sources of influence and help that add to the creating of a book. But a few stand out in my mind. At the very foundation are my many mentors as I "grew up" in the training world, especially Richard Whiteley, John Humphrey, John Bray, and Donald Somers. I am indebted to Charlotte Pollard, who got the whole project started, and to Evelyn Mareth, who encouraged me to publish. I greatly appreciate the help of Whit Rummel and Len Edwards, who shared their wisdom about video in training, and that of Jennifer Potter Brotman, Paul Jarvie, and Dorothy Yep, who shared their time and thoughts with me when I drew a blank or needed feedback. And an emphatic thank you is due Sue Dutton, who always helped me find the missing piece of the puzzle when my ideas failed to fall into place.

P A R T

1

A STEP-BY-STEP GUIDE TO DEVELOPING TRAINING PROGRAMS

1

GATHERING INFORMATION ON TRAINING NEEDS

DEFINITION

The first step in the design and development of a successful training program is finding out about the people to be trained and the type of training they need. This process, and the information you gather, is usually called a Needs Analysis. The information comes from a variety of sources and usually includes data on the program's content, the instructional method or methods used, and other questions of implementation.

IMPORTANCE

The Needs Analysis provides the information you need in order to decide on the objectives, content, and format of the program. You document this information in Step 2 when you prepare the Program Specifications Document. A relevant, accurate, and complete Needs Analysis ensures that the program will be useful to participants and help them improve their performance.

EXECUTION

Sometimes the program sponsor does the Needs Analysis even before a training professional becomes involved with the project. In that case, your task as training professional is to review the process and the results. You need to be sure that a valid training program can be built on the information. Below I outline a plan for designing a Needs

Analysis. In reviewing a finished Needs Analysis, you can use the same process to measure its effectiveness. If you doubt the validity of either the process or the information, you may decide to confront the sponsor and recommend that additional data be gathered. This is an important decision. A program that fails because it is constructed on an inadequate Needs Analysis hurts not only the organization but the training professional as well. This is true even if he or she was not involved in the Needs Analysis. Therefore you may want to protect your credibility by gathering additional data. Of course, this should be done with a minimum of criticism of the existing Needs Analysis.

If the Needs Analysis has not been done, then your first step will be to design a Needs Analysis plan. The plan should outline clearly

- what information you will gather
- who you will get the information from (or where, in the case of documents)
- what methods you will use to get the information
- what the final summary or interpretation will look like

There are many methods of gathering and interpreting information about training needs. To put together your plan, you will find it helpful to think about the following six questions first:

1 Should a Needs Analysis be done?
2 What information do I need to design the program?
3 What are the best sources available for the information?
4 What is the best way to get the information needed from the sources?
5 How will I compile, analyze, or summarize the information?
6 How and to whom will I give the information?

Thorough and thoughtful answers to these questions will allow you to put together a Needs Analysis plan that produces the information you need to design a high-quality, relevant program.

Question 1. Should a Needs Analysis be done?

In answering this question, decide first whether or not it is ethically and organizationally appropriate to gather data at all. In cases where you feel the data are not going to be used appropriately, you may feel that the process of gathering data will do more harm than good. Whatever your final decision, the answers to the questions below will help you decide and give you important background information about the project.

- Has the target population (the people to be trained) been clearly identified?
- What are the sponsor's objectives in having you gather the data? Does the sponsor simply want to promote his or her own political visibility? Does he or she want the data to support reorganizations, terminations, or recruiting? Identify motives like these early. In some cases, they may so undermine your attempts to gather information that it is not worth your undertaking the project. It may hurt your reputation to participate.
- How will you proceed if the data you gather show that the problem the sponsor wants to treat with training is due to lack of motivation, inadequate support, poor recruiting, or some other condition that training cannot alleviate? How will those identified as responsible for the problem react? Will you be blamed for such unwelcome data?
- If training is needed to solve the problem, has the sponsor made it clear that he or she will actually develop a program? If data are gathered but no action is taken, your credibility may suffer.
- Does the program sponsor have a predetermined set of needs to be addressed? If so, how will the sponsor respond if these are not the needs you uncover in your Needs Analysis? If the sponsor intends to address his or her predetermined needs regardless, then it is important that you ask why the sponsor is having you do the Needs Analysis. Is there danger of your participating in just a token data-gathering project that will not really influence any training effort?

It is important to understand all the reasons for doing the Needs Analysis and all the potential outcomes before you establish a plan or take any action. You do not want to dwell on possible negative outcomes. However, sometimes an answer to one of the questions above will cause you to discontinue the project. Many training programs fail because their sponsors' expectations or motives were not originally understood and therefore could not be dealt with effectively.

Question 2. What information do I need to design the program?

It is critical to identify all the information you need without gathering extra information that serves no purpose. Start by examining the sponsor's reason for wanting to develop the program. For example, if the impetus for the program is "supervisors' failure to follow legal guidelines when terminating employees," then it is essential to gather information about the supervisors' knowledge of the legal guidelines. It is probably not essential to gather data about how supervisors run their staff meetings, unless early information indicates that there is some connection. Of course, once you have established what information you are looking for, you will still want to remain open to new avenues of inquiry if they seem connected to the topic.

It is also critical in gathering information to ask specific questions. General conceptual information about training needs is almost impossible to address in concrete training experiences. For example, if the Needs Analysis indicates that "supervisors don't seem to understand the legal guidelines," it is still unclear what training is needed. But if you ask "*Why* don't they understand the legal guidelines?" you may find that it is because of the language of the handbook, or because they never have a chance to practice applying the guidelines, or because two different handbooks say different things, or even because organizational practice differs from legal guidelines. Only then are you ready to design a training program to help solve the problem.

At this point, keep in mind that there are two broad categories of needs that are usually met by training programs. One is *training needs*. These are the skills and knowledge that are necessary to perform in one's present position. The other is *development needs,* the skills or knowledge that will be needed for performance in a future position or at a later time. In this chapter, I talk primarily in terms of training needs, but most points will apply equally well if you are identifying development needs.

There are a number of topics about which information may be gathered in a Needs Analysis. You may want to ask questions only about the specific area being studied (e.g., "product knowledge," or "terminating employees"). On the other hand, you may want to ask questions about the whole job if the program is meant to improve overall skills. Here are some typical questions.

1 What is the *job* of the target population (either in the specific
   area of concern or in general, if the program is to improve over-
   all skills)?
2 What do the members of the target population *actually do* in
   their jobs?
   How do they use their time?
   With whom do they interact (both in the company and outside)?
   Whom do they report to?
   Whom do they manage?
   How is their performance measured?
   What is a typical day/week for them?
   How are they trained? recruited?
   What is a typical background for a person in their group
   (school, previous work, personal background)?
3 How does the employees' actual work or performance differ
   from the job they were expected to do (or are envisioned as
   doing in the future)? In other words, what is the gap between
   what is required and what is actually being done?
   Why does the gap exist?
4 What are the typical situations, customers, products, or projects
   that these people deal with? (This is good information for the
   Needs Analysis now and will also be useful to you in writing
   program materials later on.)
5 What are the important issues, problems, or changes these people face at the present time?
   What is the "history" of the department, including turnover and
   changes in leadership style?
6 What skills, knowledge, and behaviors do the members of this
   group need to acquire or to improve upon in order to do their
   jobs better?
   How can they best be acquired?
7 What factors are there that may affect efforts to train this group
   (for example, attitude, schedule, past training efforts, management support or lack of it)?

Question 3. What are the best sources available for the information?

The best sources of accurate information, whether a person or a
document, should all first be identified, even if some of them later

on prove to be difficult or impossible to use because of expense, un-availability, unwillingness, or the like. Wherever possible, seek several sources for the same information so that the information will be well balanced. Listed below are most sources of information.

People
- members of the target population
- their managers
- upper management
- subordinates of the target population
- co-workers or peers of the target population
- human resources personnel
- vendors to the organization
- customers
- competitors
- industry experts or observers
- business experts (in areas such as management, strategy, training, etc.)

Documents
- recruiting records
- written reactions to past training
- job descriptions
- samples of work
- exit interviews and turnover records
- past studies, analyses, or surveys of the target population or their jobs
- other training programs used for this or similar target populations
- performance appraisal records
- union grievance records or other legal records
- procedures, handbooks, or other job aids
- papers typically used by the target population in doing their job (i.e., order forms, customer correspondence, project reports)

Question 4. What is the best way to get the information needed from the sources?

There are many methods and combinations of methods available for collecting data. Here are some common ones.

Open-ended or closed questionnaires. Open-ended questionnaires are composed primarily of questions for which there are many possible answers or interpretations. For example, an open-ended questionnaire might include such questions as "what factors influence productivity in your area?" or "how do new people learn their job in your department?" Respondents write in their responses. Closed questionnaires are composed of questions with a limited number of responses. For example, a closed questionnaire might include such questions as "How often do you sit down with your subordinates to discuss their performance?" — a)once a year; b)once a month; c)once a week; d)less than once a year. Respondents simply choose one of the responses offered. It is also possible to combine open-ended and closed questionnaires. In that case, the initial questions are closed, but there is room for open comments at the end.

Individual or group interviews. These are face-to-face meetings in which the interviewer asks questions of one or several people. The questions are usually established in advance, but additional questions or topics can be introduced as the interview progresses. The interviewer takes notes on the responses of the interviewee(s).

Observation. This involves a trained person observing the potential trainees on the job. The observer may be asked to note what the potential trainees do on the job, what they need to do on the job, job conditions, key events on the job, or other factors.

Analysis of existing documents. This involves a study of written materials that may contain information required by the Needs Analysis. The examiner finds out what relevant information the documents contain, notes that information in writing, or copies parts of the document.

Each method has its own unique characteristics, which can affect the cost, quality, and quantity of the information obtained. So before you choose a method, be sure you know who is going to be using the method to collect the data. Most methods require some experience or expertise and so should not be assigned to anyone simply because they are willing to donate their time. (A possible disadvantage of a particular method, therefore, might be a lack of trained personnel.) You may need to train the people you do have to use the method effectively.

Here are the major advantages and disadvantages of each method.

ADVANTAGES

DISADVANTAGES

Open-ended questionnaires
- allow respondent to introduce new topics
- may uncover important data not asked for
- are less work to prepare (you don't have to foresee possible responses)

- are difficult for those respondents who have trouble expressing themselves in writing
- makes respondents more reluctant to commit on paper (harder to be anonymous)
- are harder to answer (you must categorize answers)
- afford no way to probe further
- require time and thought from respondents
- depend on recall

Closed questionnaires
- are easier to answer
- are easier to analyze (the use of a computer reduces cost)
- yield more precise information
- are more anonymous

- require more skill and work to prepare
- are limited in scope and subtlety
- may bias the respondents' answers
- afford no way to probe further
- do not allow for unusual answers

ADVANTAGES	DISADVANTAGES

Individual or group interviews

■ can pick up more information from tone, personal appearance, or expression	■ require skilled interviewers, especially for group interviews
■ are flexible and allow questioner to probe further where needed	■ may make people uneasy
	■ may reflect the interviewer's biases
■ can build commitment in interviewee(s)	■ are time-consuming and can reach only a small sample
■ may provide insights in interviewee(s)	■ are expensive if travel is necessary
	■ are more difficult to analyze
	■ may cause group interviewees to influence each other

Observation

■ yields data that are not skewed by recall or interpretation	■ often requires some knowledge of the job
	■ does not always reveal attitudes
■ can bring out subtle things hard to express in interviews or questionnaires	■ can interfere with work
■ can be a good way to gather data for course materials later on	■ can require time to see all aspects of a job, making it an expensive technique
■ can build rapport with the target population	■ may influence what happens (by observer's presence)
	■ reveals what is, but not necessarily what should be

Analysis of existing documents

■ can get data from several sources in one place, cutting time and cost	■ may produce uneven data, skewing final information received
■ seldom involves travel	■ can consume analyst's time without producing results
■ may be able to use some previous analysis of the data	■ may not cover all areas needed
■ doesn't depend on commitment of others	■ takes skill (to pick out the right information)

Questions 5. How will I compile, analyze, or summarize the information?

The answer to this question depends on what type of information is gathered and on the method used.

Obviously, the type of information you gather determines whether your final report will be analytic or subjective. If you collected numbers and had respondents categorize their answers, then you can do more analysis, projecting trends or conclusions based on the sample. If, on the other hand, you collected examples and incidents, then you will be drawing general conclusions which you will support with examples.

The methods of gathering data, listed above, have a significant impact on the way you analyze the data. For example, with closed questionnaires, responses can be coded and summarized in numerical terms. With interviews or open-ended questionnaires, the final information will be more subjective, since you must categorize certain types of responses.

If a computer is used to analyze the data, you must identify the exact analysis you wish to do in advance, so that data can be coded accordingly. In addition to standard tabulations of responses, cross-tabulations — breakdowns into cross-referenced categories — can bring out interesting data. For example, in addition to tabulating "the average number of years account executives have been with the company," you might also want to know "which regions have the longest average tenure for these people." Such cross-tabulations, however, must serve a clear purpose, or you may have "data overload."

Content analysis.   Sometimes it is necessary to compile or summarize a large quantity of nonnumerical data, often from a number of sources. In this case, a process known as *content analysis* is helpful. An outline of this technique follows.

1 Read all the data over once quickly. Jot down major themes or word groups that jump out at you (i.e., "politics," "pressure," "teamwork").

2 Read the data a second time, jotting down apparently related ideas under the themes identified in the first reading. Add

themes if necessary. Important comments that don't seem to fit into any one category may be labeled "leftovers" and noted in a separate place. At this time, try to use the exact words or phrases used in the data. You may want to note the sources of the comments. Do this by coding the comments according to their source (e.g., code remarks from Manufacturing with "M," from Finance with "F"). This will allow you later on to see if trends or themes are related to the source of the comment, or if the theme seems to cross group lines.

3 Now try arranging themes (with their related comments) in different ways. Try switching comments among theme groups. Experiment with fitting leftovers into various categories. If new themes emerge at this time, add them. If a theme seems to be no longer needed (because all comments under it fit into other themes), discard it. Theme groups may also be combined or divided into two at this point. Be sure you don't have any theme groups that are so large that they begin to lose their meaning.

4 When theme groupings seem to make sense, read the data again. Have any important points been left out?

5 As you start to work with the final theme groups, you may find further need to rename, divide, and so on. In a Needs Analysis this could be because one theme group proves too difficult to teach all at once, or two themes cover similar learning points, or an important point gets lost when it is inside a larger theme group.

   NOTE: Some people find it easier to go through the data and identify all key words first, without trying to identify any themes or groupings. Then they go through the list of words all at once and let major themes emerge naturally.

   Whatever technique you use, be sure you have a clear picture of what the final information will look like before you begin to gather data. In other words, do you want to end up with statistics, anecdotal information, lists of problems, or something else? Otherwise, you may find yourself wanting one kind of analysis but having the information only to produce a different kind of analysis. Finally, once you decide how you will compile and summarize the information, be sure your plan agrees with the sponsor's expectations about the type of analysis or summary to be produced.

Question 6. How and to whom will I give the information?

The results of the Needs Analysis will be documented in the Program Specifications in Step 2. However, they may also be presented to the sponsor in either a more comprehensive or a more concise form, depending on the sponsor's needs. This separate presentation does three things. First, it allows the sponsor to ask questions and to be sure he or she understands the data. Second, it tests the degree to which the sponsor accepts or rejects the data. Third, if the sponsor is not yet ready to move to a Program Specifications Document, or even to commit to a training program, the presentation of results can motivate the sponsor to move ahead and take action.

You may make your presentation either orally, with visual aids as appropriate, or in written form. A written presentation may include a detailed report along with a summary of the major results, often called the Executive Summary. In either case, include an overview of the way the data were gathered and analyzed. It is also important to distinguish between objective information coming directly from your study of the situation and the subjective conclusions that emerged from your study of the data or from your participation in the research.

Always think through and prepare your presentation with care. If time or your sponsor's attention is limited, present only the major conclusions you have drawn from the data. You can share the details on request or in a later, comprehensive report.

You may wish to present the data to other parties, such as the participants in the Needs Analysis, other human resource professionals, or other management groups. The degree to which this information will be shared with any non-sponsors should be agreed upon with the original sponsor of the Needs Analysis.

All of these options for presenting your data should be brought up with the sponsor before the Needs Analysis begins. You want to know in advance exactly what the sponsor expects to receive from you and in what form.

REMEMBER

The Needs Analysis is often done just as the sponsor and the training professional are forming a relationship. Therefore it is tempting to

---

REQUIREMENTS

Materials: Questionnaires; Interview Guides; Observation Guides; documents to be studied. Any background material needed by interviewers, observers, and other participants, so they may familiarize themselves with the target population and their jobs.

People: Selected members of the target population to be studied. Interviewers; observers; developers of questionnaires; administrators; analyzers.

Time: Varies greatly depending on the methods to be used.

Budget: Expenses of preparing and distributing questionnaires. Expenses for facilities and travel connected with interviews or observation.

Facilities: Quiet facilities for interviews.

---

cut corners or leave differences of opinion unexplored in order to avoid jeopardizing that relationship. It is the quality and thoroughness of the Needs Analysis, however, that will determine the ultimate success of the training program. No amount of writing and design can save a program that is being developed to fill the wrong needs. Therefore you must face all necessary issues at the Needs Analysis stage, to ensure the ultimate quality of the training program.

Even more alluring is the temptation not to do a Needs Analysis at all, particularly when the sponsor tells you that he or she is already quite sure what the needs are. Or there may, in fact, be times when some previous research has already produced the information you need. In either case it is important to first establish just what information is needed; then decide whether the existing data will fill that need. Often, it will not. Once again, failure to insist on thorough needs research at this stage will only cause problems later. By that time, your credibility and budget may already be in jeopardy.

LOOKING AHEAD

You have now collected the information you will need to design a relevant, useful program for the target population. The next step is to document that information in a form the design team can use to run the design meeting. Step 2 will show you how to produce that document, called the Program Specifications Document.

2

PREPARING THE PROGRAM SPECIFICATIONS DOCUMENT

DEFINITION

In this step, you must document the information about training needs gathered in Step 1, and the information provided initially by the sponsor, for use by the design team. The Program Specifications should provide all information necessary to design the program. When ready, the Specifications are first given to the program's sponsor or other line management groups who need to approve its content and format. Once approved by the sponsor or sponsors, this document is distributed to the people who will participate in the design meeting, Step 3.

IMPORTANCE

The Program Specifications Document is the driving force of the design process. It provides a common reference point throughout the design meeting. You will use it during the meeting to test whether the final design meets the original requirements of the sponsor.

As a written document, it can be reviewed and approved by the program sponsor. This provides an important checkpoint, ensuring that the program, as designed, has the content and form envisioned by its sponsor. Sometimes the results of the Needs Analysis in Step 1 are not what were expected. The preparation of the Program Specifications then gives the sponsor a chance to come to terms with the results. The sponsor can then decide whether the program should address the needs uncovered, the content originally envisioned, or some combination of the two.

The Specifications Document also puts in written form certain "musts" and "nice to haves" which may have been indirectly expressed. These may include such factors as who will instruct the course, where it will be held, or the preferred learning methodologies. In the Program Specifications, such constraints are brought out in the open and acknowledged by everyone before the design effort begins.

EXECUTION

The Program Specifications Document typically has four parts:

1 Program Background
2 Description of the People to Be Trained
3 Program Objectives
4 Program Requirements and Constraints

Let's look at each in detail.

Section One: Program Background

This section describes why the program is needed, who is sponsoring its development, and how the program fits in with the organization's overall training effort or business strategy. It may also explain any historical or cultural factors that may affect the program. For example, you might describe a former training program involving the same people and the reasons for its success or failure. This section might help the design team understand why this program is now a priority or why it will have high visibility. You may also explain why certain management groups have a stake in the program, and describe upcoming changes in the status or role of the people to be trained. These are all critical factors to be aware of as the design effort begins.

Section Two: Description of the People to Be Trained

This section contains a description of exactly who will attend the program, often called the target population. It should first describe the future participants in terms of the criteria by which they are chosen to attend. These criteria may include level, title, function, skill level, future assignments, past experience, or current interests.

Most important, this part of the Specifications describes the gap between the skills and knowledge of the target population and the skills and knowledge required by their present jobs. In some cases, the program is part of an ongoing development effort and is not meant to address any particular gap or deficiency. In that case, the population description will generally describe the current skills or knowledge level of the people and the skills or knowledge they will require in the future. The information in Section Two explains why the program objectives in Section Three have been chosen.

You should also include anything about the population characteristics that may have an impact on the training. For example, you might point out that these people are not accustomed to formal training, describe the population's historical bias against marketing techniques, or explain why it is difficult to free these people for long periods of time.

Section Three: Program Objectives

This is the heart of the Program Specifications Document. It actually describes what the program should accomplish. In this section, you may describe first the broad intent of the program, such as "to improve the product knowledge skills of the salespeople." But you must also specify exactly what new skills and knowledge the program participants will have after the program that they did not have before. For example, one program objective in a product knowledge program (see sample at the end of this chapter) might be "participants will be able to make a knowledgeable presentation about all of the twelve major products." Another might be "participants will be able to answer any of the common questions asked about the U–15 Condenser without referring to a product manual."

For most programs, however, there are far more possible objectives than there is time to address them. So it is imperative that the design team know which objectives are to be accomplished in this program. The priority of these objectives may not be readily apparent from the Needs Analysis done in Step 1. The Program Specifications Documents needs to establish those priorities for the design team. Therefore, part of writing the Program Specifications is interpreting the Needs Analysis and working with the sponsor to decide which objectives are to be addressed. If the program objectives are not clearly outlined in the Program Specifications Document, they will have to be chosen at the design meeting. This is not a good use of the design team's time.

Section Four: Program Requirements and Constraints

This section describes the requirements and restrictions that will affect the nature of the program design. For example, this section might point out that the program cannot be longer than two days or that it must include follow-up activities that involve the participants' managers. It might outline the locations in which the program must be deliverable or limitations about the kind of equipment that can be used. It might also specify that interactive methodologies be used or that participants work primarily with their own back-home situations.

The characteristics of the program addressed in this section of the Program Specifications may include, but are not limited to, the following:

- budget
- program length
- number of participants
- locations for delivery
- deadlines for development
- instructor qualifications/limitations
- need to be modularized
- practical vs. conceptual focus
- relative emphasis on topics
- learning methodologies
- prework
- evaluation
- follow-up
- link to other programs, systems, or conceptual frameworks used by the company (for example, performance appraisal)
- guest appearances or presentations by non-instructors
- obligatory social activities attached to program

Typically, people focus on the Program Objectives section of the Program Specifications. In many cases the other sections are not even written up. But, to design a program that will meet the sponsor's needs and the needs of the population, all four sections are important.

REQUIREMENTS

Materials: The results of the Needs Analysis done in Step 1, whether in the form of written notes, tapes, questionnaires, or an initial analysis.

People: The project manager is usually responsible for preparing the Program Specifications Document, although the actual writing may be delegated to someone else. The project manager may work closely with those who participated in the Needs Analysis in order to compare conclusions and interpretations. The project manager also works with the program sponsor or other line management groups in getting their approval of the Specifications or in making the changes asked for by those groups.

Time: One-half day to two days, depending on the volume of data to be summarized. Additional time may be required to meet with the sponsor or other line management groups.

Budget: No special requirements, unless an external consultant is used.

Facilities: No special requirements.

The sample Program Specifications Document found at the end of this chapter is shorter than most such documents, but illustrates their general shape and format.

REMEMBER

If the design team includes non-training professionals, the packet sent to the team members with the Program Specifications may also include materials that will help those people become familiar with training terminology and methods. These might include a glossary of training terms, articles on adult learning or training methodologies, and samples of design documents that will allow non-trainers to understand what the end product of the design meeting will look like. Design Documents are described in detail in Step 4.

The Program Specifications Document should be written in simple, specific language. For example, a statement like "the program must be implementable in a variety of settings with regard to technological support" may not be helpful to the design team. It would be far more helpful to say "the program must not use any advanced technical equipment such as videotape or computers since it will often be given in branch offices which do not have such equipment."

Send the Program Specifications to the design team well in advance of the meeting. Tell them the document should be studied before the design meeting. Encourage people to contact the project manager if they do not understand the document or disagree with its major points. In this way, confusion or disagreements can be cleared up before the design meeting instead of during it.

When sending out the Specifications, you may also want to outline the agenda of the design meeting. The design team will then understand, when studying the document, how it will be used and what will be expected of them at the meeting.

When outside training consultants are used, the information in the Program Specifications is often found in the client's request for a proposal. In other situations, the client gives verbal information for the Specifications to the consultant, who then documents it in his or her proposal. When this is the case, the program sponsor should carefully review and approve the proposal, in lieu of the Program Specifications. The proposal can then serve as the driving force for the design meeting.

LINE REVIEW

This preparation of Program Specifications is the first of three major points in the design and development process when a line review is essential. When the Specifications are complete, it is very important that the program sponsor or other line management groups involved review the progress of the project so far. As we mentioned above, this is done by the sponsor or other groups reviewing and approving the Program Specifications Document. It is very important that their review of the Program Specifications is a thorough one. Otherwise, the design team may find itself working with specifications that are inaccurate or unacceptable to the program sponsor, and the design meeting will simply be lost time.

LOOKING AHEAD

You have now organized all the requirements of the program in one clear document, and those requirements have been confirmed by the program sponsor. You can now turn your attention to the design meeting itself. Step 3 will show you how to prepare and conduct that meeting, using the Program Specifications as the common reference point.

Exhibit: 2A

SAMPLE OF PROGRAM SPECIFICATIONS
FOR
PRODUCT KNOWLEDGE PROGRAM

Section One: Program Background

As our organization has diversified its activities over the last five years, the number of products each salesperson must understand and present to customers has grown rapidly. In light of the recent decision not to use salespeople dedicated to selling only certain products, the Marketing Department feels it is essential to improve the product knowledge of the sales force. In discussions with the National Sales Manager, it has become clear that he supports such training. However, he has made it clear that he will send his salespeople only if the program has a highly practical focus. He feels that past product training in the company has consisted primarily of the Marketing Department's giving long technical presentations, in which they "blew their own horn," an approach which he feels is not worth his people's time out of the field.

Section Two: Description of the People to Be Trained

This program would be open to all salespeople, both new and experienced. In time, it could become a mandatory program. Once most salespeople have attended, sales support people would be allowed to attend.

At this time, the salespeople tend to be very skilled at gathering data from customers. However, once the data are gathered, salespeople tend not to recognize many of the customers' needs which the organization can actually meet. Instead, they tend to recognize only those needs met by the core products which the company has offered for more than three or four years. This tendency is reinforced by sales managers who sold only those core products when they were in the field, since those were the only products in existence at that time.

When needs that can be filled by newer products are mentioned by customers, salespeople tend to say nothing, or they indicate that our company cannot be of help in that area.

The company's salespeople are very reluctant to spend time out of the field. Their managers are equally reluctant to schedule them for activities that detract from sales time, unless such time has a clearly practical payoff.

Section Three: Program Objectives
At the end of this program, participants will

- be able to recognize, during data collection, any needs that the company is capable of addressing with its products
- be able to give an initial description of all products in terms of the benefits they offer to the customer
- be able to use the product guides in order to prepare a detailed presentation for a customer or to answer detailed questions about the product
- know who to call in the marketing department to arrange for a joint sales call or for help in preparing a detailed presentation on a product

The execution of paperwork, once the product is contracted for, will not be addressed in this program. This task is carried out by sales support personnel, and salespeople can refer questions to the customer service representative assigned to the account.

Section Four: Program Requirements and Constraints
Because of the factors described above, the program must have a clearly practical focus. It should

- provide opportunities for salespeople to work with real sales situations they bring to the program
- be highly interactive, with opportunities for the participants to practice using the knowledge and skills introduced
- be fast-paced, with few social activities or leisure time periods
- be taught by instructors who either have been or are currently in the field

The program should not include any segments in which the Marketing Department "blows its own horn." Instead, the program should focus on (1) providing salespeople with helpful tools and opportunities to practice using them in real sales situations, and (2) the use of the Product Guides, which are now being developed.

3

CONDUCTING THE DESIGN MEETING

DEFINITION

In this step, training professionals meet, either independently or with non-trainers involved in the program, to determine the overall content of the program and the content and instructional methods to be used in each unit of the program.

This step serves as a bridge between Steps 2 and 4. The Program Specifications (Step 2) are the driving force in the design meeting. After the meeting, the results are written up in a Design Document (Step 4). This document then provides the blueprint for the development of program materials.

IMPORTANCE

The design meeting ensures that everyone involved with the program examines together its overall flow, methodology, and content. Decisions can be made in the light of the overall needs of the program rather than the needs of any one unit. Everyone's opinion can be aired and points of disagreement settled before development begins.

If individual parts of the program are developed separately, without an overall design, they may not fit smoothly together. They may even contradict each other or overlap. Learning activities may repeat each other, general themes may not be smoothly integrated into the program, and transitions between units may be choppy or nonexistent.

The overall design that emerges from this meeting is the foundation for the remaining steps. Therefore it is critical that your thinking be thorough and logical. If you overlook important considerations, there can be major problems later in the development process and with the quality of the final program. For this reason, allow plenty of time for the design meeting. The right people must attend, and you should encourage everyone to share his or her views and defend them if necessary. All involved parties should prepare thoroughly.

EXECUTION

I. Preparation for the Meeting

1. Decide how much time is needed. There is no hard and fast rule, but in general, you will need from two to four hours of meeting time for each day of training to be designed. More time is generally needed if

- the subject matter is complex or not normally taught in training seminars
- the participants are sophisticated in training methodologies and, therefore, have high expectations
- the program developers are relatively inexperienced in program development
- the program will be highly visible or controversial in the organization

2. Select attendees for the design meeting. Attendees may be selected from any of the following groups:

- sponsors of the program
- line managers who have knowledge of the target population
- members of the target population
- subject matter experts, from either inside or outside the organization
- experts in training design, from either inside or outside the organization
- people who will be involved in developing the program, such as writers or reviewers
- future program instructors

The interactive process used in the design meeting suggests that the optimal number of people is six to eight. However, the project manager must make a trade-off between having too many people and having the right people. If the group is larger than eight, then much of the work in the meeting may be done in two smaller groups. Under no circumstances should there be more than twelve people.

There are several guidelines for determining who should attend. First, look at the clarity and complexity of the Needs Analysis data. If the needs for the program are unclear or complex, you will want to involve line management or members of the target population. Their knowledge can fill in holes in the data and help determine priorities of needs.

Next, consider the need for line management commitment. If the managers of the target population will need to reinforce the program back on the job or encourage attendance at the program, then those managers should be represented at the design meeting. In this way, they can understand and commit themselves to the program objectives in advance.

Consider also the complexity of the program itself. If its content or design is probably going to be complex, then, if at all possible, the people who will work on the development should attend the meeting. Otherwise, you will have to repeat the discussions and the rationales behind decisions made at the meeting.

Finally, think about the technical content. If the program content will be highly technical, subject matter experts will probably be needed at the meeting. Development people will also need to attend to receive the technical background they will need. Future instructors might want to attend for the same reason.

After all these factors have been considered, a well-balanced design meeting team might consist of

- the project manager
- a representative of the sponsor or line management
- one or two members of the target population
- a development person
- a training design expert

3. Notify meeting attendees.   As long as possible prior to the meeting, tell them the purpose of the meeting and the date, time, and place. Let them know about any prework requirements and tell them whether the Program Specifications Document is attached or will be sent later.

4. Send the Program Specifications Document to meeting attendees. They should receive the document far enough in advance for them to study it carefully.

5. Develop a meeting agenda.

6. Determine and communicate responsibilities for the meeting. Decide who will be responsible for taking notes in preparation for documenting the design in Step 4. Decide who will carry out other assignments steming from the meeting.

II. The Design Meeting

1. Opening the meeting. The leader (usually the project manager) should establish a productive climate. This is done by first reviewing the purpose and objectives of the meeting. Then the leader asks participants to share their expectations and any hestitations or special objectives they may have. The leader must make it clear how the meeting will be run and why that process is important. This is the appropriate time to reinforce the importance of using the Program Specifications as the guide for the design process. The meeting leader should, at this time, ask participants for any questions or initial reactions to the Program Specifications, which they have reviewed.

2. Designing the overall structure of the program. The first design task of the meeting is to take the topics from the Program Specifications Document and group them according to content. Generally, each group of related topics will correspond to one unit of the program. For example, a unit might be designed to address tardiness; or a unit may address a related group of discipline problems, including tardiness, absenteeism, unacceptable language, and improper dress.

You should then establish the topical flow of the program. In other words, you decide in what order the topics will be treated, allowing for logical transitions from one topic to another. The flow should also support the general theme of the whole program.

3. Designing the individual units.   The second task of the meeting is to design the individual units one at a time. First, establish the objectives of each unit — in other words, decide exactly what should be taught in relation to that topic. For example, if the topic is effective meetings, do you want participants to be able to (1) recognize a good meeting, (2) prepare for a meeting, (3) actually hold a good meeting, or (4) understand the consequences of negative meetings? Any of these objectives is valid. From among all the possible objectives, the group must decide which ones are appropriate for this unit in this program. This is obviously a key decision in terms of the methodology that will be used and the results that the unit will produce.

Next, establish the learning points of each unit. What are the three or four key points the participants should take away from the unit? Experience has shown that participants can only absorb a few points at a time. If priorities are not set, then participants will be so overburdened with learning points that they will absorb none. Setting priorities is often difficult, since everyone in the design meeting will have his or her favorite points on the subject. Obviously, the choice of learning points will depend in large measure on the choice of objectives.

Next, establish a methodology. The question to ask is "Which learning methodology will best accomplish our objectives?" In the case of a unit on meetings, if the objective is to have participants understand the negative results of a bad meeting, then a simulation or group role-play may create the kind of experiential learning that is needed. On the other hand, if the objective is to help the participants plan effective meetings, then a task force working on a meeting plan might be the best methodology. Discussions of various methodologies and the appropriate use of each are found in Part Two.

At this point, you may identify existing materials that will meet the objectives established for this unit. These may be materials created earlier for your organization, or they may be materials available from a training vendor or another training organization.

It is critical, however, to *be sure these materials really meet your objectives*. It can be very tempting to use materials because you have used them successfully before, because others find them effective, or because they would be easier or less expensive and *almost* do the job. Be sure existing materials are exactly on the mark before you build them into your design. Then treat them just as you would new materials. When testing your design, scrutinize their fit with the rest of the program. Test them against your design in Step 8. Use the critical parts in your Materials Test in Step 9. Never *assume* that the materials will work in this program because they have worked in other programs. Your objectives may be completely different. And materials only work if they work with the objectives of *this* program.

Choosing the objectives, learning points, and methodologies will be your most important decisions in the design meeting. Other decisions (timing, setting, discussion questions, or examples to be used) can be made later if necessary. But deciding on the objectives, learning points, and methodologies will involve important priorities and trade-offs, and all points of view on these issues should be considered immediately. Therefore these decisions must be made at the design meeting where all perspectives can be represented.

4. Testing the design. The final task of the meeting is to test the design against several standards. Does the program flow logically? Have any of the decisions made about unit designs caused the original flow to be impossible or ineffective?

Considering the psychological needs of the participants, you should also ask

- Is the material relevant to the participants?
- Is sensitive or confidential information handled in a way that participants can be comfortable with?
- Is a variety of learning methodologies used to prevent boredom or repetition?
- Is a need to learn created in each unit?
- Are opportunities provided to build trust with others, if that is required by the program?

The design should also be tested to see if it meets participants' physiological needs. Ask

- Are there sufficient breaks and free time?
- Are there sufficient changes in physical locations and types of activities?

- Are there lively activities after meals or at the end of the day, to combat natural low-energy times?
- Are normal attention spans respected?

The design should also be tested to see if the requirements and constraints outlined in the Program Specifications have been respected, and if the topics specified have been addressed.

In general, make sure your design meets the established criteria for effective training programs. Experience has shown that most successful training programs have certain common characteristics. Accordingly, test your program to see if it

- starts from a clear statement of program objectives
- presents an appropriate number of topics or ideas for the time available
- employs a logical flow and clear transitions between topics
- provides for the participants' psychological and physiological needs
- employs a variety of appropriate learning methods
- provides opportunities for participants to assess their current level of proficiency in or awareness of the topics and ideas presented
- provides opportunities for the participants to draw and build upon their own experiences
- allows participants to be actively involved in the learning process
- allows participants during the workshop to apply or plan to apply the topics and ideas presented to their job situation

5. Finishing up after the design meeting. Sometimes the design team is unable to finish all of its tasks during the time allotted for the meeting. When this happens, the project manager should focus, in the meeting, on making the major decisions about objectives, learning points, and methodologies. After the meeting, the project manager can work alone or with part of the team to finish the design process. The other members of the design team will have a chance to react to these final decisions when they review the Design Document (after Step 4).

REQUIREMENTS

Time: From two to four hours meeting time per day of training to be designed.

Materials: The Program Specifications Document; the meeting agenda; any other prework materials sent out; flipcharts, markers, and tape.

People: Ideally from six to eight people, selected from

- program sponsors
- line managers
- training professionals
- members of the target populations
- subject matter or training methodology experts
- people who will develop or teach the program later on

Budget: No special requirements, unless outside consultant fees are involved. Some travel and entertainment funds may be needed if attendees come from out of town.

Facilities: Meeting room

REMEMBER

The project manager should

- take a proactive role, managing time and using good questioning, clarification, listening, and conflict-resolution skills during the meeting, as needed. He or she should encourage attendees to use good interpersonal skills such as listening, respect for the opinions of others, and openness to new ideas or alternatives.
- orient the group toward results, and emphasize the need to be realistic about what the program can and cannot do.
- be flexible if it appears that all of the expected outcomes of the meeting will not be produced. He or she should encourage others to accomplish what they can and let the group decide what tasks can be done by a smaller group or individuals later on.

- avoid putting too much pressure on the group. The project manager should be sure that the important questions (e.g., overall flow, objectives, learning points, and methodologies) have been thoroughly addressed. He or she should not push the group to make more decisions than it can handle in the time available.
- contact participants after the meeting to thank them for their work and to let them know how the project will proceed. This helps ensure their commitment to the project, should their help be needed later.

LOOKING AHEAD

Now you have a program design, most likely in the form of informal notes and flipcharts, and probably some mental notes as well. Step 4 will show you how to present this design in a thorough comprehensive document. This document will then serve as a guide to everyone involved in the remaining steps of the development process.

S T E P

4

PREPARING THE DESIGN DOCUMENT

DEFINITION

In this step, the design established at the design meeting in Step 3 is documented in a form that will serve as the blueprint for the rest of the development process. The document may take any one of several forms, depending on the complexity of the program and the development process that will be used.

IMPORTANCE

The act of preparing a Design Document tests whether the program design is thorough and detailed enough to guide the development process. If the person preparing the Design Document has trouble writing it, the issues or details that have not been dealt with become apparent. This problem can then be corrected before the development process gets underway.

The Design Document is also important because it can be studied by the program sponsor or others concerned and approved by them. In this way, everyone involved with the program can begin the development process on the same wave length. If there are misunderstandings or misgivings later on, anyone can refer to the Design Document to see just what was intended or promised.

During the development process, the Design Document serves many purposes. These include

- a source for the Materials List and Project Plan (Step 5)
- a guide for people preparing the course materials

- a reference when reviewers examine the materials to see if they support the design
- a guide for instructors preparing to test the materials or teach the pilot program, and later the foundation for the final instructor notes
- a marketing tool for explaining and promoting the program and gaining line management's commitment to send their people
- a reference point for any later redesign, either during development or later in the program's life

EXECUTION

An important decision about the Design Document is its level of detail.

In general, the document will need to be more detailed when the design of the program is complex. It will also be more detailed if there are many different people involved in the development process. The more people involved, the more such a central reference document is needed, to keep everyone on the same track.

When writers or other development people are inexperienced or unfamiliar with the subject of the program, the Design Document will also be more detailed.

A more detailed Design Document is also indicated when the program will be widely implemented or will be used over a long period of time. If implementation is wide, a detailed document will be necessary to keep the design on track as different people work with it. If the program will be used over many years, then the detailed document will guide redesign or updating efforts later on in the program's life.

A sample Design Document excerpt appears at the end of the chapter. A typical Design Document first describes the overall flow and objectives of the program. It then describes each unit, including the objectives, the timing, what will happen during each activity, and the learning points to be taken away by participants. The document may also describe the specific discussion or presentation points to be made during each activity and even the settings of cases, role-plays, or other materials. The Design Document may also include a diagram of the course flow and daily schedules.

A more complex Design Document, in addition to the information described above, may break each unit into different segments. For

---

REQUIREMENTS

Materials: The Program Specifications Document; notes and flipcharts from the design meeting.

People: The project manager is responsible for the preparation of the Design Document. However, the actual writing can be delegated to a member of the design team. Sponsors or other management groups will also be involved in the review and approval of the Design Document.

Time: Depends on the form used. In general, preparation of a detailed Design Document takes up to half the time the program will require to run. For example if the program will be two days, the Design Document will require up to one day to prepare. Additional time may be required to discuss the document with the sponsor and make any changes needed.

Budget: No special requirements, unless an outside consultant is used.

Facilities: No special requirements.

---

example, one segment may describe the introduction to an exercise, the next segment what happens when the participants actually do the exercise, and a third segment the wrap-up discussion. The document then describes each segment in terms of media used, timing, objectives, teaching process, and detailed content. In this more detailed Design Document sometimes called a storyboard, the exact setting or content of materials are usually spelled out, and the discussion questions or points of emphasis are specified.

A more detailed Design Document may not be as effective as a marketing tool or a checkpoint with sponsors. But it is an excellent basis for detailed instructor notes. And it provides a wealth of detail for inexperienced development people or people working with an unfamiliar topic.

Regardless of the exact format chosen, the Design Document for any major program development project should include

- the overall flow of the program and arrangement of units
- the objectives of the program and of each unit
- the methodology and activities to be used in each unit
- the timing of each activity
- enough detail about the activities to enable others to identify the materials needed and to prepare those materials

REMEMBER

To test your Design Document, you should examine it from several perspectives. First of all, ask yourself if the document is detailed enough so that writers, reviewers, and instructors can each do their job when the time comes. In other words, will writers be able to tell what their materials should look like? Will reviewers have enough information to see whether the materials prepared carry out the intention of the design? Will instructors for the materials test and the pilot program have enough information to prepare their teaching notes?

If your program uses some materials that already exist, check that those materials and their use has been adequately explained in the Design Document. You may be familiar with the existing materials, but people using the Design Document will need all the same information about existing materials as they will about new ones.

Next, ask whether the document answers all the questions a sponsor or line manager might have if they were sending their people to the program.

Now, ask whether the Design Document will allow developers to see how any proposed changes will affect the overall program design.

Finally, ask if the document is detailed enough. Consider the experience level of the developers, their knowledge of the program content, and the number of people who will be involved in development. Also consider the projected use of the program in different locations or over a long period of time.

There is no point in preparing a Design Document just to say that one exists. If a Design Document cannot fulfill its purposes, then it is not worth your time and effort putting one together. Therefore it is important that you test your Design Document to see if it is a solid blueprint for the rest of the development process.

LINE REVIEW

Step 4 is the second of three steps during the design and development process when line review is essential. When the Design Document is complete, it is critical that the sponsor and other line management groups review the progress so far. The most efficient method at this point is for the concerned parties to study the Design Document and give you their reactions. Make sure the sponsor or other groups have really reviewed the document in depth and have not given it just a cursory look. If you suspect that the document has not been studied carefully, you may want to insist on an in-depth discussion. Failure to uncover misunderstandings or differences of opinion at this point will hurt everyone in the project later on. In some circumstances, the project manager can even ask the sponsor for a written "sign-off," indicating that the program described in the Design Document is indeed the program wanted.

LOOKING AHEAD

You now have a document that will guide each step in the development process, saving many hours of explaining the design or briefing others involved with the program. You are now ready to organize the development activities. Step 5 will show you how to do that using two key documents, the Materials List and the Project Plan.

Exhibit: 4A

EXCERPT FROM
A DESIGN DOCUMENT

Unit 2: Feedback Meetings

At the end of this unit, participants will

- know how to document indications of good and poor performance
- have practiced preparing for a feedback meeting
- understand the importance of periodic feedback meetings with subordinates and how they differ from day-to-day supervision
- know the steps to use in a feedback meeting
- have practiced running a feedback meeting for one of their own subordinates

The unit will be conducted as follows:

1:00–1:30   Lecturette and discussion: Feedback meetings

The instructor presents the idea of developing subordinates through feedback meetings. These meetings are defined as discussions between supervisor and subordinates, in which the employees' overall strengths and weaknesses are identified and future development is planned. The payoffs are emphasized as follows:

- a reminder of the work group's overall goals and each employee's role in their achievement
- a means of getting employees involved in discussing their future
- an opportunity to reward achievement, stress opportunities, and give employees encouragement and direction
- a chance to identify problems and air grievances

In the course of this discussion, the instructor guides participants in identifying why it is so hard to hold these meetings and why supervisors avoid them.

1:30–1:45   Group discussion: Preparing for a feedback meeting

The instructor describes how to collect performance data on an ongoing basis. Emphasis is on preparing for a feedback meeting by collecting indicators of good and poor performance throughout the performance period, not just in the few days preceding a meeting.

Participants discuss how to collect such data. The instructor makes the point that a feedback meeting is much less threatening for the supervisor when he or she has been collecting information on a regular basis.

1:45–2:00   Individual exercise: Preparing for a feedback meeting

Participants record observations concerning the overall performance of one of their subordinates, thus preparing for an actual feedback discussion with that subordinate. The observations and a meeting plan are entered in the participants' Planners.

2:00–2:45   Trio-group exercise: Sharing preparation plans

Participants work in small groups to share the preparation they have just done for a feedback meeting with a real subordinate. Each participant has 15 minutes to present his or her analysis and receive feedback and additional ideas from other group members.

2:45–3:00   Coffee break

3:00–3:30   Lecturette and video model: The feedback meeting

The instructor introduces a step-by-step model of how to hold a feedback meeting. Then the instructor shows a videotape in which these steps are shown being used well. The steps will include, but not necessarily be limited to, the following:

1 Explain to subordinate why and how the meeting will be run, using a positive tone.
2 Allow subordinate to express general feelings about how the job is going.
3 Review both positive and negative evidence of performance, using specific examples of each.
4 Answer any specific questions the subordinate has about his or her performance, and make sure he or she understands your answers.
5 Discuss ways of improving in less successful areas of performance and decide on action if needed.
6 Discuss subordinate's work preferences and goals in the orga-

nization, making it clear that you want his or her input but cannot make any promises.

In discussing these steps, the instructor will emphasize that the tone of the discussion should be matter-of-fact and that it should be made clear to the subordinate that such meetings are routine, not an indication that something is wrong.

The instructor leads a discussion of the steps and clears up any questions or misunderstandings about them.

3:30–4:15   Role-play exercise: Feedback meetings
Working in groups of three, participants take turns playing the roles of supervisor, subordinate, and observer in three different role-plays, with each participant playing the supervisor in the real-life situation he or she analyzed earlier. The group discusses each role-play, identifying how the steps were used and what could have been done differently.

4:15–4:45   Group discussion of role-play exercise
Participants and instructor discuss the role-plays. They note what helped the meetings and what seemed to hinder them. The class identifies obstacles to good feedback meetings and generates ideas for dealing with them.

4:45–5:00   Individual exercise: Personal planning
Participants work in their Planners to identify ways in which they can do a better job of holding feedback meetings with their subordinates.

5

PREPARING THE MATERIALS LIST AND PROJECT PLAN

DEFINITION

In this step, two important planning and monitoring tools are created. Using the Design Document written in Step 4, the project manager creates the Materials List, which identifies all the materials needed to conduct the program. The project manager then identifies all the activities required to develop and test the program materials and the people responsible for those activities. This information is documented in the Project Plan. The two documents are distributed to everyone connected with the development process and updated regularly to reflect the current project status.

IMPORTANCE

The Step 5 documents are a bridge between the planning steps 1 through 4 and the implementation steps 6 through 10. Step 5 translates the information in the Design Document into a form usable for tracking and managing the development process. Both the Materials List and Project Plan guide the efforts of the program material writers. The documents also help the project manager plan and control the time schedule, often tight, between program design and implementation. The Materials List continues to be used by program administrators and instructors throughout the life of the program.

The preparation of the Materials List and Project Plan is often the only stage at which the project manager views the project as a whole. From now on, different people may work with parts of the project. The entire project will only come together again at the pilot session.

Therefore the project manager must give Step 5 his or her full attention so that the documents produced are complete and accurate. This will avoid having to "catch up" later on.

Step 5 does not end when the Materials List and Project Plan have been generated. It is critical to update these documents as the project moves ahead so they always reflect the current project status. The use of outdated documents by some project members can create confusion and bad feelings. Even more serious, it can cause omission of materials and failure to meet deadlines.

EXECUTION

Materials List

For each piece of program material required, the Materials List should include:

1 *A code number for the piece of material and the number or name of the unit in which the piece is used.*
2 *A description of the piece* (e.g., "Case: John Greene (A)"; "Task Force Instructions: Environmental Implications"; "Role-Play Exercise: Instructions for Subordinate #1"). The description must make it possible to differentiate this piece from other pieces used in the same unit. Each separate piece of material should be listed separately. In other words, all materials for the role-play exercise should not be listed as one item called "Role-Play Materials." Instead, they should be listed as separate items, such as "Role-Play: General Instructions," "Role-Play: Observer Instructions," and so on.
3 *The person who will write or develop the piece.* In the case of materials that already exist, this is the person who will obtain the materials and double check that they are appropriate, complete, and of good quality.
4 *The date when the piece will be ready for review.*
5 *Comments.* This category is important because it allows room to include important information that may otherwise go unnoticed. It might concern the content of the piece, sources of information for the piece, interim deadlines to meet, or reminders about special requirements.

REQUIREMENTS

Materials: The Design Document from Step 4; any documents that contain the schedules of project team members.

People: The project manager is usually responsible for developing both tools. Although the physical task can be delegated, many project managers prefer to do it themselves, in order to become thoroughly familiar with the project.

Time: A minimum of one to two hours for each document, not including production time. Additional time will be needed to update the documents periodically.

Budget: No special requirements.

Facilities: No special requirements.

Once the program is implemented, the information in points 1 and 2 above can serve as a guide for inventory and shipping of program materials.

A partial sample Materials List is shown at the end of the chapter.

Project Plan

The Project Plan can take many forms. But it should always include:

1 *All the steps necessary to move from the program design stage to the final pilot session.* When in doubt, the process should be broken into more steps rather than fewer steps. Whenever steps are lumped together, no matter what the logic, some smaller steps may be forgotten. You may even find it necessary to put together an overall plan with the major steps, then break the plan down into sub-plans for use at different stages of the project.

   For example, the overall plan might read "prepare for Materials Test." But the people executing that step will need a more detailed list of what needs to be done, such as "decide on items to be tested," "set objectives for each test," and "brief instructor for test."

2 *The primary person responsible for executing the step.* The plan may also list other people who will assist in carrying out this step and describe their exact responsibilities.

3 *The deadline for the step to be completed.* The plan may also indicate the time period during which the step will be performed. For example, the plan may state that research for materials will be completed by August 31. But it might also indicate that this research will be carried out from August 5 to August 31.

4 *Comments.* As in the Materials List, this space allows the noting of important information that might otherwise not be shared or kept in mind.

A partial sample Project Plan is found at the end of the chapter.

REMEMBER

As the Materials List and Project Plan are prepared, the project manager should set up a schedule or process for updating them. You may decide to do this on a date basis (e.g., every two weeks; once a month) or on an event basis (e.g., after every project review). Someone should have the clear responsibility for these updates. Between official updates, this person will track all changes on a master copy, which is available for everyone's reference.

Be sure to include in your Materials List such nonwritten materials as audio-tapes, video-tapes, prepared flipcharts, overheads, and diplomas or mementos given at the end of the program.

In developing the Project Plan, be realistic. Build in "slack time" to allow for less controllable activities such as review by others or outside production.

Prepare now for possible delays. Decide what activities can safely use short cuts to make up for delays in other areas. Identify which activities can be sped up if necessary by using additional resources.

You may feel that time pressure from the sponsor or others makes it necessary to commit to an unrealistic project plan. But if you do feel the plan is unrealistic, you should consider confronting the issue now rather than waiting until deadlines are missed. Once you have missed a deadline, your arguments may be interpreted as just an effort to cover up your own poor performance.

LOOKING AHEAD

You have now translated the Design Document into an action plan for developing the final program. You also have a Materials List that will tell you what materials still need to be developed. In Step 6 you will take the first step in implementing your action plan when you gather information needed to draft the program materials.

Exhibit: 5A

SAMPLE MATERIALS LIST (EXCERPT)

MATERIALS	WRITER	DUE DATE	COMMENTS
Module 1:			
1. Case Study: Knowing the Job	MH	September 13	Don't use DP setting
2. Instructions for Ind. Exercise	EN	September 20	
3. Planner for Ind. Exer.	MH	September 22	
4. The Planning Maze	ST	September 6	3–5 situations
5. Answers to Maze	ST	September 6	Include rationales
Module 2:			
1. Overview of Coaching	NW	September 6	
2. Introduction to Role-Play	NW	September 6	
3. Role Instructions: Mgr., Sub., Obs.	NW	September 6	

Exhibit: 5B

SAMPLE PROJECT PLAN (EXCERPT)

ACTIVITY	PERSON RESPONSIBLE	DATE TO BE COMPLETED	COMMENTS
Develop Needs Analysis interview guide	HR	March 15	Include questions about new performance appraisal system
Identify interviewees and schedule interviews	SS & HR	March 30	Nominations already requested from department heads

ACTIVITY	PERSON RESPONSIBLE	DATE TO BE COMPLETED	COMMENTS
Hold interviews	HR & WH	April 10	
Compile interview results and compare results of each interviewer	HR & WH	April 15	D. Linstrom will review

6

GATHERING INFORMATION FOR PROGRAM MATERIALS

DEFINITION

In this step, information needed for the program materials is gathered. This information, either from written sources or from interviews, usually comes from inside the organization. But in some cases outside sources may be used. You may be looking for procedural information such as the process used in auditing an account, or conceptual information needed for strategic planning. Or you may be looking for background information and examples from the workplace. This information will help the writers prepare cases, roleplays, and other materials that reflect the real world of the participants and allow people to "try on" new skills or procedures in a realistic context. Sometimes the earlier Needs Analysis interviews will have already provided considerable perspective on the situation and a sufficient supply of anecdotes. In that case, Step 6 can be shortened or omitted.

IMPORTANCE

This step ensures that the program materials reflect the reality of the participants' workplace and that the examples and cases used are relevant. This realism encourages participants to accept the learning points of the program. Sometimes the settings and examples to be used have been established in the original design. In that case, those choices can be tested during this step for appropriateness and changed if necessary. Because it involves other people in the organization, this step can also create interest and support for the program.

EXECUTION

I. Preparation for the Interview

1. Decide what information you need.   The kinds and amount of information will, of course, depend on the materials you are going to produce. You should have in mind exactly what form the final materials will take. For example, will you produce a checklist for a good meeting plan, or do you want only an overview piece on the elements of a good meeting?

You should also consider any information you already have. This may include information from the Needs Analysis, from your own knowledge of the organization, or from other sources. Then you can identify the information you still need to gather. Be specific in defining what information you want. This will make it much easier to determine what questions to ask in an interview.

2. Select your sources.   These will be either written documents (e.g., recruiting records, performance reviews, strategic plans) or people you need to interview. In either case, the specific sources should be chosen according to several criteria.

In the case of documents, ask yourself whether they will contain the information you need. Will the information from these documents be credible? Then determine whether the documents are available. Think about what you will need to do to get to the documents and extract the necessary information. Now you are in a position to choose the documents you will use as sources.

If your sources are people, you will first want to think about who has the knowledge or perspective you need. Ideally, some people will have multiple perspectives, which they can share with you. Then consider whether these sources are credible. Are they willing to be interviewed? Will they be honest and forthright? An understanding of or experience with training can make someone a valuable source, one who may better understand what you are trying to accomplish. If the source has prejudices or blind spots, determine what they are so that you will not be misled by them.

3. Determine what questions to ask.   This pertains primarily to interviewing. To conserve time and get the information you need, make your questions specific and clear. If you have already determined exactly what information you need, this should not be difficult.

Since you do not know what answers you will receive, you may need to prepare several paths for the interview, depending on the information you get in the beginning. For example, you might be planning to build a role-play about a subordinate who is not careful enough in preparing reports. However, if your first few questions establish that this is not a common problem, you may have to take another path and gather information about another type of problem.

The way in which you phrase a question can often have a dramatic impact on the quality of the information you receive. Be sure to prepare open, imaginative questions. For example, if you want to identify the most serious problems in running meetings, you could simply ask what those problems are. On the other hand, you might get more information by asking the interviewee, "When you think about the next meeting you are going to run, what do you imagine as the most terrible thing that could happen at the meeting?" Try to avoid questions that can be answered yes or no.

4. Set up interviews. If someone else is to choose the people you are to interview (using criteria you established), he or she should understand exactly what you are looking for. For example, if you ask for people to interview for a program on manufacturing safety, you may have in mind people who have been involved in problems stemming from safety violations. But unless you make that fact clear, you may find yourself interviewing only people known for their good safety records. Do not set up interviews of less than one hour. You will need that much time to build rapport, provide background, gather information, explore alternate subjects, and summarize.

5. Gather background information. Your credibility will be enhanced if it is evident to the interviewees that you know about their job, their background and experience, the current issues in the workplace, and the jargon used. Such knowledge will make it clear to them that the subject is important to you. Interviewees will probably feel more trust toward you and more comfortable discussing sensitive information.

6. Prepare a written interview guide. A written interview guide ensures several things. First, you are forced to think through your questions in advance. Second, your interview will be more consistent in form and content. Third, the guide serves as a good reminder should the interview begin to wander and not cover the subjects you are interested in.

Allow space below each question on the form so you can take notes. But don't leave so much space that the guide becomes too long and unwieldy. A two- or three-page guide is probably most useful. A sample interview guide is shown at the end of the chapter.

II. During the Interview

1. Start with an overview.   Begin by explaining exactly what you are trying to accomplish. If you are looking for general information, say so. Otherwise, it may look as though you are unsure of what you want. If you are gathering information for a specific piece of material, describe it to the interviewee. This will help him or her to give you the information you need and not stray from the subject.

Explain ground rules, such as confidentiality, note-taking, and timing. This is also a good time to confirm how much time is available for the interview. Then you can manage the time available throughout the interview, rather than rushing at the end because time has run out.

2. Begin with open, comfortable questions.   There is often tension at the beginning of an interview. This can be alleviated if you start with a general question that is nonthreatening and easy to answer. For example, you might ask an interviewee to describe how he got his job. Or you might ask an interviewee to describe a typical day in her office. As the interviewee starts to talk, respond with encouraging comments and gestures. Let him or her know that you find the information helpful and interesting.

3. Take thorough notes.   Often, when an interview is over, interviewers find that they need some information that, because it did not seem very useful during the interview, they failed to take notes on. It is helpful to take complete notes throughout an interview. Let the interviewee know at the beginning of the session that you will be taking notes. Ask if there is any objection. People often feel less threatened if you offer to let them see the notes at the end.

Tape-recording interviews is a subject of controversy. Many people feel it inhibits the interviewee. Others feel it is an excellent way to catch quotes and complicated examples. Sometimes recorded interviews don't save as much time as you may think. It takes far more time to listen to each tape than it does to review even lengthy notes. And sometimes reliance on a tape recorder makes the interviewer less attentive during the interview.

4. Try to spark ideas in the interviewee. If you have a particular example or situation in mind, or if an idea takes shape during the interview, test it with the interviewee. Many times this will elicit more information than will a standard question. Ask such questions as "Would it ever happen that . . ."; "How would it work if . . ."; "Can you describe a case when . . ."; or "Does this sound like something that might happen here?"

Never assume that you have heard everything worth hearing on a particular subject. When you finish with a subject, ask the interviewee if there is anything else you should know about that subject. Sometimes the answer to that question is the most valuable information you will receive.

Don't become committed to one idea or example too early in the interview. Even if it seems ideal, probe for additional information. You may change your mind as you hear more ideas.

Don't get tied up in technical details. If you need more details on a particular subject, you can always get them later.

5. Observe as well as listen. Look around you and observe what is happening outside of the interview. That means events before the interview and interruptions or other events during the interview as well as physical surroundings. Ask about what you see and what is happening. This may provide information that you may otherwise miss.

6. Leave the situation open-ended. Ask for permission to call the person back for more information if it is needed. But make it clear that you may or may not do so. If appropriate, ask for the names of other people you should talk to about the same topics. In both cases, be sure that you retain the option to follow up or not as needed.

7. Leave on a positive note. This interviewee could well become a supporter of the program. So leave a positive impression by

---

REQUIREMENTS

Materials: Interview guide; Design Document; outline for the materials to be written, if appropriate.

People: Selected interviewees and interviewers.

Time: At least one hour but not more than two hours per interview.

Budget: No special requirements, unless travel is involved.

Facilities: An interview site that minimizes interruptions, preferably within the interviewee's work environment.

---

thanking him or her for being available. Indicate that the person has been helpful and interesting. Offer once again to share your notes or to let him or her see the final materials.

III. After the Interview

1. Review your notes immediately.   This allows you to fill in illegible parts and to add details that were not written down. You can also add more general impressions or ideas sparked by the interview. Then try to use your notes as soon as possible while the interview is still fresh.

2. Don't be afraid to call back.   Most people are flattered to know that you are using the information they provided. So don't hesitate to call back for more details or to review the written materials with the interviewee. Additional time spent with you will surely be less irritating to the interviewee than materials that distort his or her ideas.

REMEMBER

If the interviewee is hostile or not knowledgeable, then concentrate on general topics and end the interview as early and as politely as possible.

If the interviewee is distracted or interrupted frequently, ask about the distraction or the interruptions, as a source of information. You may then want to offer to come back at a better time.

If the interviewee talks in very technical terms that confuse you, then ask global questions. Act as if you know the answer but want to hear it in his or her own words. For example, you might ask, "Why do you think your department exists?" or "Can you describe what you see as the most important changes in this process over the last two years?" These kinds of questions are often most productive when you think you know the answers. You may be surprised at what you hear.

LOOKING AHEAD

You now have the information you need for the program materials. In Step 7 you will actually create those materials.

Exhibit: 6A

SAMPLE INTERVIEW GUIDE

NOTE: This interview guide was used to interview sales managers for a role-play in which a manager gives feedback to a subordinate who has been over-aggressive in a joint sales call with his or her manager.

INTERVIEWEE: ——————————

POSITION: ——————————

Tell me about your job. (*How time spent, responsibilities, concerns*)

How did you arrive at this job? Is that typical?

Tell me about your subordinates. (*Background, talents, problems, their concerns*) Are they typical?

How do you go about calling with your salespeople? (*When, why, role each of you plays, preparation and follow-up*)

Do you typically give them feedback after a joint call?

When do you give them feedback? How do you do it? When is it hardest? Easiest?

Does it vary by subordinate?

Can you describe a recent feedback meeting with one of your sub-ordinates? What feedback did you give? How did you run the meeting? What happened in the call?

Did you feel it was a good meeting? Why not? Anything you would do differently?

How do you think that salesperson felt before the meeting? After the meeting?

Do you sometimes have to give feedback to a salesperson about being over-aggressive? Can you describe how you did that? *(Circumstances, how handled, how it turned out)*

What do you think was in that subordinate's mind before that feedback meeting? Did he/she realize what was coming?

If interviewee has not given feedback to an over-aggressive salesperson:

Does it ever happen that a manager like yourself has to give a salesperson feedback on being over-aggressive?

If interviewee doesn't hold meetings or has never had an over-aggressive salesperson:

How would over-aggressiveness show up in a call?

What would be a typical reason a salesperson would give for being over-aggressive?

What approach would you take in a feedback meeting about over-aggressiveness if you were to hold one? What would you think about before that meeting? What would you actually say?

What might a salesperson be thinking before such a feedback meeting? How might he or she respond to the feedback?

Do you have any other thoughts on feedback meetings after joint calls?

Would other people in your job tend to see things the way you do? Would they tell me different things?

Can I call you if I need more information or clarification?

Is there anyone else you think it would be important for me to talk to on this subject?

Thank you.

7

WRITING MATERIALS

DEFINITION

This step involves the preparation of the materials needed to carry out the program design. In addition to materials used by the participants during the program presentation, you may be preparing pre-work materials, follow-up materials, job aids, and content for teaching aids like pre-printed flipcharts, overheads, and slides. If the program requires non-written materials such as audio or video tapes, you must first prepare written scripts for them. The remaining steps of the development process will involve the review and testing of these materials.

IMPORTANCE

This step is critical in making the program a relevant experience that helps participants improve their job performance. The design is only a plan and requires materials of all types to implement it. When the materials are of good quality and carry out the intention of the original design, the program has an excellent chance of success.

EXECUTION

The process for writing program materials depends on the type of materials you are writing. Suggestions for designing and writing materials to support various training methodologies can be found in Part Two.

There are some general guidelines, however, which apply for any type of materials.

I. Preparation

Before you begin writing, prepare an outline for the materials, if you did not do this when gathering information in Step 6. For example, for a role-play, your outline will note what point of view each role will take, what information will be provided to each player, and what points to make in the observer's instructions. For a case study, your outline will include how the case study is to be organized, the major events or topics to include, and the perspective or time organization of the case. For a task force, your outline will include a list of the information needed by the participants and the order in which it will be presented.

Thus your outline allows you to organize your thoughts before you actually begin to write. It provides you with a clear picture of the final written piece. That picture then guides your writing efforts so that you do not ramble or get off the subject as you write. The decisions you make in preparing the outline are not ones that you should be making while you are writing.

Sometimes writers, while preparing materials, begin to question whether the materials asked for will achieve the desired objectives. You can always reexamine a program design. Sometimes you discover a better idea as you start to work with the materials. However, if you reopen the question of what materials are needed, you should discuss the matter with the design team. No changes should be made without looking at the effect of those changes on the overall design of the program.

II. Writing

Follow your outline as much as possible when you write out the materials and observe basic rules of good writing. The criteria for good writing will vary for each type of material. In exercise instructions, for example, clarity is the foremost consideration. For a case study, an interesting style will be important. For a role-play, completeness of instructions is critical. Keep in mind that, regardless of the type of material, the value of the written piece is not measured by its length. Its value is measured, instead, by how well the written materials fulfill their intended purpose and how well they fit into the overall program design.

III. Preliminary Testing

Once you have written the materials, review them yourself first. Do the materials accomplish their purpose? Are you satisfied with the general quality of writing? Sometimes, you as a writer will be blind to the faults in your product. Other times, however, you can catch preliminary problems at this stage, and you can improve your own product before passing it on to a reviewer in Step 8.

You may have technical questions at this point. If so, resolve them now so that the materials you give the reviewer are as complete and accurate as possible.

REMEMBER

Beware of creating materials that try to duplicate exactly the work environment of the participants. If the situations described are too close to the real thing, participants may be distracted from the learning issues raised. It is often advisable to use settings that *resemble* the actual organization but that are not identical. Then small differences will seem natural and will not become the focus of discussion — such as, for example, a situation in which participants try to guess the actual identity of characters described.

For the same reason, avoid technical situations that are actually present in the participants' work environment unless you are teaching technical facts or processes. For example, participants may spend their time checking the technical facts instead of dealing with the interpersonal issues raised by a role-play.

If you encounter problems in preparing materials, always go back to what you are trying to accomplish. For example, if you can't come up with good questions to ask on a role-play observer form, look back at the objectives of the role-play. If one of your objectives is to give feedback to the person who plays the manager, then on what points should that person receive feedback? What is the manager trying to accomplish? What process or skills is he or she trying to use? The answers to those questions will make it clear which questions should be asked on the observer form.

Suppose you have a case about problem subordinates, and you cannot describe the situation in enough detail to satisfy you. When you look back at the objectives of the case, you see that the design requires a case demonstrating the dangers of letting subordinate

---

REQUIREMENTS

Materials: Design Document; notes from data-gathering in Step 6; any materials or outlines prepared in Step 6.

People: The writer. Others may be consulted during the writing process if the writer needs additional information or perspective. A word processor or typist may be required to process the material.

Time: Depends on the type and quantity of materials being prepared. Do not underestimate the time required to write up apparently simple materials such as exercise instructions.

Budget: No special requirements.

Facilities: No special requirements.

---

problems go untreated, *not* a case that illustrates how to solve such problems. You need to describe the consequences of the situations, not ways in which they might be solved. Therefore the detail you were seeking is not really needed. Thus you put your writing back on track by referring to the case objectives for guidance.

LOOKING AHEAD

You have now created the materials needed to present the training program. In Step 8, a person with another perspective will examine these materials to see if they accomplish the objectives of the program design and if they are well written.

8

REVIEWING MATERIALS AGAINST THE DESIGN DOCUMENT

DEFINITION

In this step the written program materials are reviewed against the Design Document to see if they will perform the function intended by the design. They are also reviewed for general quality of writing and interest. One person, usually someone other than the writer, performs this analytic task. He or she reviews the materials, then meets with the writer to review any problems and discuss possible solutions. The project manager or other design person may also attend this meeting to offer a second view and additional suggestions.

IMPORTANCE

This step is an important checkpoint before the materials are sent to the line for their reaction. If the line's technical review is done before the materials clearly fit the design, then the line may have to see the materials again after any problems have been resolved. Step 8 also avoids sending the line badly written materials that give a mistaken impression of the quality of the course, an impression difficult to undo later. At this stage, you can catch basic problems with the materials before time and energy are expended for Step 9, a Materials Test involving many people. Then, during Step 9, you can concentrate on identifying the problems that the test participants will uncover.

EXECUTION

Remember, you are reviewing the materials (or having the materials reviewed by someone else) for two reasons: first, to see whether the materials meet the specifications of the Design Document. For example, suppose the Design Document calls for a task force exercise that is intended to give participants confidence in using a new performance appraisal system. You will review the exercise to see if it will, in fact, create confidence. Is all the necessary information provided so that the experience will be a "win"? Is the task clear, and is enough time allowed so that the quality of the results will make participants feel good about their work?

Second, look at the general quality of the writing. If it is already clear that there are major problems with meeting the design specifications, don't spend time on the quality of the writing until those design problems have been cleared up.

If you are reviewing more than one unit of a course, each unit's materials should be reviewed separately, so that you can concentrate on one set of objectives and issues at a time. As a reviewer of materials, you will go through the following steps.

Step A. Read the part of the Design Document that relates to the materials you will review. If you are not familiar with the program, you will need to become familiar with the entire Design Document at this time. You should also consult any preliminary outlines or scenarios for this material, which were established after the design meeting.

Step B. Read the materials over quickly, jotting down first impressions in the margins or on a separate sheet of paper. For example, your comments might include such items as "melodramatic," "not clear who is boss," "too negative," "final result wanted is not clear," or "why is this question on the observer form?"

Step C. Read the materials again and modify or amplify your comments if needed.

Step D. Refer back to the Design Document and decide whether these materials do what the document intended. You will need to think about how the materials will be used. Do the materials include all the necessary information? Will most participants react the way the design requires them to react? Put yourself in each participant's place at this point and ask what your reaction would be.

For example, suppose the design requires a role-play that allows participants to practice disciplining their employees. You will look at whether the role-play as written describes a discipline situation similar to those the participants usually encounter. You will also look at whether the situation described requires the skills participants need to practice. Does the feedback form give feedback on those skills?

Another design might require that participants discuss a variety of ways to handle a customer complaint. You will then want to look at whether the case study makes participants see a variety of possible approaches. Is the case relevant and real, and will it make people eager to share their views?

If the Design Document established questions the instructor will use to stimulate discussion, then use those questions to review the materials. For each question, jot down the answers that naturally emerge from the materials. Are those the answers or issues the designers intended to have emerge? For example, in the customer complaint case, one of the questions might be "How do you think the customer feels?" You will want to jot down the answers participants would probably come up with after reading that case. Are those the points the designer wanted to bring out? If not, the case needs more work.

If the design requires certain results from an exercise, look at the instructions and jot down the likely results. Are they the results required? In the performance appraisal task force described earlier, the desired result might be a presentation that identifies the key stages of a performance appraisal meeting. So read the instructions and ask yourself if you, as a participant given this assignment, would be likely to come up with those results.

This is the key step in the review process and should be performed very carefully. Some trainers believe you can test whether the materials serve the design only in a real program session. But, in fact, many problems can be identified simply by carefully examining the materials. This avoids wasting time and energy on several pilots. It also avoids serious public relations problems when the first session or sessions do not run smoothly.

Step E. If design fit problems are minor, review the materials now for quality of writing. At this time, you will be looking for such qualities as realism, clarity, subtlety, consistency, and liveliness. Many of these, of course, are essential to good writing. But often the qualities to look for depend on the type of materials being reviewed. A description of important qualities needed in different types of materials is found in Part Two.

Step F. Now that you have identified any problems with the design fit or the quality of writing, decide on specific suggestions for solving them. These suggestions will be very helpful when you meet with the writer. The more specific your suggestions are, the more helpful they will be.

Step G. If, at this point, you are unsure exactly how to define a problem or how to solve it, you may want to share the materials with another training professional and get a second opinion.

Step H. Share your reactions and suggestions with the writer, but remember that the purpose of this step is not to give him or her a performance review. Be sensitive to the need for both positive and negative feedback. Focus on how the materials do or do not perform their function, not on the generic skills of the writer. This means organizing your feedback around the type of action needed rather than around the faults identified. Make this meeting a joint problem-solving session in which your objective is to help the writer identify what action needs to be taken. If another design person attends this meeting, the writer should welcome that attendance. The third person's role should be to give additional ideas, not to add or reinforce criticism.

Step I. At a later time, review the revised materials to see if the problems have been resolved. This second review should be standard procedure, so that the writer does not feel you are "checking up" on his or her ability to make the changes. This final review is essential, because there are frequently misunderstandings during the first feedback session. As a result, problems may be only partially solved and further feedback and problem-solving may be needed.

REMEMBER

Reviewing is a highly subjective process. If the writer disagrees with your reactions, don't hesitate to involve other design people in the discussions. The most valid interpretation is often a combination of several different viewpoints. The focus should always be on how the materials will best serve the design of the program, not on whose opinion is "right" or "wrong."

As you review the materials, remember to put yourself in the place of the participants. Concentrate on how these materials would make you feel as a participant. Would you react with a desire to defend your opinion? Would you be intrigued by the task to be done? Good, if these reactions are intended. Materials that initially appear to be excellent may have serious faults when viewed within the context of the design they should serve.

If there are problems both with the design fit and with the writing, try to solve the design fit problems first. The writing problems may then no longer exist or can be dealt with after the design fit has been established.

LINE REVIEW

Step 8 is the last of three steps in the design and development process when a line review is essential. At this point the line reviews the materials primarily for their technical accuracy and the degree to which they reflect the participants' world. Therefore, this review may actually be done by line people different from previous line reviewers. Before, the line looked at the purpose and overall content of the program. Now, you want line people who can verify the accuracy of the materials without necessarily concerning themselves with the overall design. The program sponsor may also want to review the materials to see if the general tone is appropriate and to identify any political or confidentiality problems or any points where "hypothetical" situations are too close to true ones.

Too often, trainers rely only on the line to review materials. But you cannot count on the line reviewers to identify design fit problems. Line managers do not usually have the expertise necessary to see how materials will work in the classroom. They can only test those points mentioned above. For example, a line manager may feel that a case study is an excellent description of the work environment.

REQUIREMENTS

Materials: Design Document; any preliminary scenarios or outlines for the materials to be reviewed; the drafted materials to be reviewed.

People: Reviewers; writers; any other design people the writer or reviewer might ask to be involved.

Time: Depends on the type and length of materials. Average is about one hour to review the materials for one unit. Additional time is required for the feedback meeting with the writer.

Budget: No special requirements, unless an external consultant acts as a reviewer.

Facilities: No special requirements.

But that same case may, in fact, not bring up the appropriate issues. It is the training professional who must assess how the materials will work as training materials.

LOOKING AHEAD

You have now tested the materials for those problems that can be identified without a live audience, and the problems you found have been fixed. In Step 9, you will try these materials out on a group of actual participants, in order to identify any further changes needed in the materials.

9

CONDUCTING THE MATERIALS TEST

DEFINITION

In this step, the major program materials are tested in a classroom setting with a group of people drawn from the future target audience. The materials are tested for those points that could not be observed in the materials review in Step 8, such as accuracy of timing, participants' reaction to sensitive issues, and actual results of task force work or role-plays. Problems that emerge can then be dealt with before the pilot sessions of the program.

IMPORTANCE

The value of a materials test cannot be overemphasized. In Step 8, the materials have already been analyzed for design fit and quality of writing. But the materials test allows you to observe reactions that only actual participants can give.

If you fail to conduct a materials test and go right on to the pilot, two things may happen. First, participants may not provide an accurate general reaction to the program, because they are distracted by problems with the materials or by too-frequent requests for feedback. Second, participants may return to the organization with a negative view of the program, based on these superficial problems. That negative view may be difficult to change later.

A materials test is presented as a test. Therefore participants tend to have a positive reaction, because they view the test as an attempt to raise the quality of the materials.

EXECUTION

I. Before the Materials Test

1. Decide what is critical to test for each set of materials. Usually, you will want to test those points in the program where there is a probability of having problems when actual participants use the materials. These will vary depending on the design and the type of materials. For example, you might have to test a case study to determine whether or not the issues emerge clearly. A particular task force exercise may need to be tested for clarity of instructions or to see if the task assigned can actually be accomplished by typical participants. A discussion outline might be tested to measure the strength of participants' resistance to the topic.

Materials that are quite different from those used in previous programs will require more thorough testing than materials similar to those used in the past.

2. Determine how each piece of material will be tested. Once you know what you want to test about each piece of material, then you can decide what activity will be required. For example, will you want the participants to actually perform the task or only read the instructions and give you their reaction? Will you want to run the first ten minutes of a group discussion or the entire discussion? Will the test of a role-play require only doing the role-play or will it also include holding the final feedback session using the observer forms? Once these decisions are made, you will know how much time will be required for your test, and you can then make up a schedule. Usually, one-third to one-half of the time of the actual program is needed for the materials test.

3. Decide what information you will seek when debriefing participants. Based on the decisions made about what materials you are testing and why, you can now formulate the exact questions you want to ask in debriefing the participants on each part of the materials test. Focus these questions carefully so that you will receive the information and reactions you need and not be distracted by irrelevant topics.

4. Select and invite test participants. In selecting participants, strike a careful balance between typical participants and ones who can give you thoughtful responses and suggestions. When in doubt, err in the direction of inviting people who are supportive of training and of this project, who are articulate and outgoing, and who will be enthusiastic about attending.

Make it very clear in your invitation what the materials test is, how it will be run, and its importance to the final quality of the program. People should not arrive at the test thinking that they are actually attending the new program.

In addition to the participants, you will need an instructor and someone, often the writers of the materials, to monitor the session and take notes. Other design people may attend the test if they wish. The instructor may be a member of the design team or an outside instructor. But the test of each set of materials should not be conducted by the writer of those same materials. The writer is seldom objective enough to give the materials a fair test and is better used as an observer and note-taker. Several instructors may be used for the same test if necessary.

5. Prepare for the test. To prepare for the test, you will need to provide the instructor(s) with information about the design and about what is to be tested and why. The instructor will then prepare as for any training session.

6. Prepare the materials for testing. Even if you are testing only selected parts of the materials, all materials should be available. Sometimes you end up using materials you did not plan to use. Materials can be draft copies but should be legible and accurate.

II. During the Materials Test

The Instructor does the following:

1. Welcome and thank the participants. Explain to the participants the importance of their help and feedback. Describe how and why the program came into being and what steps have been taken so far in its development.

2. Describe how the test will be run. Explain first that they will be seeing only parts of the program. Warn them that the instructor may change activities in midstream. Exercises may start in the middle or end early. Point out that this lack of closure may cause some frustration and ask for their patience.

Tell the participants that you will ask for feedback at very specific times and that the rest of the time they should act as real participants would. Ask them to jot down their reactions or questions during the test for reference during the feedback period.

Explain that the materials may contain typos, misspellings, or unclear points. They will have a chance to mention those problems during the feedback.

3. Position each set of materials before testing. Explain exactly how this unit will be run normally. Then explain which part of the process you are now going to run.

If possible, test the materials in the same order in which they appear in the program. Begin each test by explaining clearly to participants where these materials occur in the program. Tell them what participants typically will have done and felt prior to this part of the program and what will happen to participants afterward.

4. Run the test for each set of materials. As you run the test, remain open to various outcomes. You will probably want to "manage" the process less than you would in a real program so that you can see what the participants will naturally do in an activity. Do not end a test early just because it is going well. Flaws in the materials can appear just as often in the final moments of the unit as in the initial portion.

Be sure that someone takes detailed notes throughout the test. Even information that does not seem important at the time may later serve as the basis for analyzing or solving a problem. If the notetaker includes only points he or she thinks are important, useful information may be lost.

5. Debrief the participants for each set of materials. First make it clear to participants that they should now play the role of critic. Begin by asking for their overall reaction but move quickly to the specific questions you established before the test. Be very specific in asking for the participants' feedback. Typical questions might be "Is this piece technically accurate?"; "Could this situation occur in your work environment?"; "Did you have all the information you needed to do this exercise?" When problems are identified, probe carefully for detailed reactions or descriptions of what is wrong. Focus on what effect the problem had on the participants. Then ask for specific suggestions about what would be more helpful to participants.

At this time, your objective is to gather information and ideas. You should not be choosing solutions or committing to any one course of action. An idea that sounds ideal during the debrief may turn out to have a negative side. An unorthodox idea, which you are tempted to reject out of hand, may contain the seeds of an effective solution. Therefore concentrate at this point on collecting information rather than on making decisions. Make this clear to the participants so they do not see your lack of decision as a rejection of their ideas.

Do not defend the design or the materials during this debriefing. There will be time later to assess the validity of the negative points made. To defend the program now will waste time and may make participants reluctant to speak up.

6. Thank participants. When all of the tests are complete, thank participants again for their help. Emphasize how much their feedback will affect the final program. Let them know what the next steps are in the developmental process. Ask for any final comments or reactions before ending the session.

III. After the Materials Test

1. Hold the debriefing as soon as possible. Discuss the test while the event is still fresh in your mind. If possible, everyone who observed the test should attend the debriefing. Be objective and calm about the problems uncovered and how they might be treated. The final chapter in Part One contains some useful guidelines about how to avoid excessive corrections in a program.

REMEMBER

Sometimes you are unable to use potential participants for the materials test. This may be due to logistics, to the small size of the total population, or to other problems. Try very hard to overcome these obstacles. If all else fails, the next best solution is to use people who closely resemble the population. You might use people who used to

---

REQUIREMENTS

Materials: All the participant materials that will be used in the program; any job aids or instructor materials needed to test the materials; enough copies of the materials for all participants and observers.

People: Enough participants to simulate the interaction intended by the design, usually ten to fifteen people; instructor for each part of the test; the writer of the materials to be tested, who usually acts as an observer and who will take notes.

Time: Varies according to the materials to be tested. Normally the test requires one-third to one-half of the actual program length.

Budget: No special requirements unless an outside consultant is used to conduct the test. Some travel or catering costs may be incurred if coffee or meals are provided or if participants come from other locations.

Facilities: A training room and equipment adequate for the size of the group and the methodologies used in the program.

---

be in the target population, who will be in the target population, or who have worked closely with those in the target population. As a last resort, use training staff and spend the first part of the test briefing them on the characteristics of the training population. It is preferable to hold a materials test in this way than not to hold one at all.

Listen carefully to what participants have to say during the test. In Step 8, the materials review gave you an opportunity to evaluate the materials according to professional design criteria. The materials test is an opportunity to measure participant reactions. The participants are an excellent source of ideas and feedback and you should not disregard their ideas just because they do not have training experience. They do know what they felt and learned using these materials.

LOOKING AHEAD

You have now tested the materials to the greatest degree possible before the pilot session. You have taken action to resolve the problems uncovered. In Step 10, you will present the entire program and see how it works as an overall training experience for the people for whom it was designed.

STEP

10

HOLDING THE PILOT PROGRAM

DEFINITION

In this step you will conduct an actual pilot program. This first full session of the program is attended by participants from the actual target population and usually uses finished materials. Sometimes audio or video tapes are not made until after the pilot, to avoid expensive remakes of these materials. In that case, written scripts are generally used for the pilot session.

IMPORTANCE

The pilot session serves as the final test of the program design and materials and is the first time that certain aspects of the course can be tested. These aspects include overall flow and transitions, relevance of course content to participants, and applicability of "back-home" planning and follow-up activities. The pilot program can serve several other purposes as well. Instructor notes can be generated from notes taken at the pilot. Future instructors can attend the pilot to see and participate in the program before learning to teach it. The program designers will receive detailed feedback about the program for the first time from people who have experienced it.

The pilot program may meet other objectives unrelated to the design and development process. It provides an opportunity for publicity and visibility for the program and those involved in its development. The pilot allows management to make a visible statement of support for the program through physical appearances and in other ways. In presenting the pilot session, be sure these non-development objectives do not take precedence over the design objectives.

EXECUTION

The pilot session is the most visible step in the design and development process. It creates the organization's first impression of the program, an impression which may be difficult to change later. Therefore, the preparation, presentation, and follow-up of the pilot program should all be carried out with great attention to detail and quality.

I. Preparation for the Session

1. Finalize materials.   An issue at this time is whether or not to edit the materials prior to the pilot session. If you believe there will be major changes after the pilot and if the existing materials are reasonably presentable, you should probably wait until after the pilot to incur the expense of editing. If the materials appear sloppy or hard to use, however, it is worth editing now. Appearances are important at a pilot session. For the same reason, if the material is going to be presented in artwork covers or notebooks, that artwork should be ready for the pilot if at all possible.

2. Choose participants.   This is a critical step in preparing for the pilot and should take place long before the final steps of the design and development process. Several points should be kept in mind in choosing participants. First, the participants should be typical of the target population, representing all groups or characteristics in even proportion. Second, the group should not include participants with obvious special agendas. For example, do not include participants who have been vehemently opposed to the program or to the content. Avoid participants whose performance or future career prospects are not good.

Try to ensure that most of the participants are receptive to training efforts in general and to the program being piloted. To generate future support for the program, include people whose opinion is respected and who may influence others to attend the program. Do not, however, limit your group to those people.

To ensure a true test of the program, you will want to include people representing a range of knowledge, training experience, and effectiveness in group experiences.

As with any program, avoid putting managers and subordinates in the same group if the program involves trying new skills or sharing views and feelings on sensitive issues.

Once you establish the criteria for participants, be sure that these criteria are clearly expressed to those who will be choosing the pilot group. Then remain closely involved in the choices. You may want to use a more detailed application or background sheet than usual to allow you to screen participants. Obviously, the degree to which people are willing to send the candidates you want will depend on the support you created for the program in earlier stages of development.

Sometimes the choice of participants for a pilot is left until the last minute, so that you end up with people chosen because they were the only ones available. Not only does this method give you a poor mix of people, but those participants generally sense why they were chosen. This does not put them in the best frame of mind for the program.

When participants are invited to the program, be sure they know exactly what they have been invited to and why. Try to send out a written description of the program, or have a member of the development team talk with each participant in advance about expectations and concerns. In talking about the pilot to participants, do not overemphasize their role as evaluators. You want them to approach the session as typical participants, not as part of an experiment.

All of these actions are designed to ensure that you have a typical but committed and receptive audience for the pilot session.

3. Decide on evaluation process. Even though your organization may have a standard evaluation process, you should consider a special process for the pilot program. You may want to use evaluation forms that are more detailed than usual, in order to pinpoint areas of the program that need further work. You may want to have a verbal debrief session after the written evaluations have been completed. You may also want to do follow-up interviews after the session is over.

Some trainers like to stop and ask for feedback, verbal or written, at various points during the program. This process provides ongoing feedback and allows for revisions on the spot. However, it can also confuse participants and force them into the evaluator role so that they do not react to the program as normal participants would. A compromise method is to ask for interim feedback only if a major problem seems to be present.

All of the feedback and evaluation methods you intend to use should be well established before the pilot session begins. Otherwise, participants may become confused, and the evaluation tools may not be carefully thought out.

4. Choose and brief instructors. The instructor or instructors should have been chosen long before this point in the process. In any event, they should now be thoroughly and accurately briefed in preparation for teaching the pilot. Because the designers and developers have been so involved in the project, it is not uncommon for them to assume that the instructor has knowledge which, in fact, he or she does not have, and, therefore, they fail to provide the instructor with needed background and guidance.

If the instructor has not been involved in the design process up to this point, he or she should receive copies of all the relevant design materials, particularly the Program Specifications and the Design Document. Before giving these documents to the instructor, be sure they are up to date and include all design changes.

The instructor should be brought up to date on what happened during the materials test and about any changes made. Any teaching notes from the materials test should be shared with the instructor. The instructor should also have someone available to answer questions and to discuss any areas of confusion that emerge as the instructor prepares for the pilot session.

5. Decide about other attendees. Think carefully about the attendance of other people at the pilot session. If future instructors attend, they should act as full participiants. This is the best way for them to really understand the program and the experience of the small group and individual activities. It also allows the future instructors to interact more with participants and receive more feedback on how the program is perceived.

Other observers should be kept to an absolute minimum. A crowd of observers in the back of the room, no matter how good their reasons for attending, inhibits the interaction in the classroom. If management people or sponsors want to be visible, encourage them to kick off the session or to drop in for the wrap-up or during breaks when they can talk informally with participants. Be absolutely sure that management observers are not present during sensitive sessions, such as discussions of back home problems on the job or receipt of personal feedback. You will never see the true impact of such sessions if participants are tailoring their comments to people in the back of the room.

At least one member of the design team will, of course, attend the pilot. If instructor notes need to be written, the design team representative can prepare them, based on the pilot session and using the Design Document as a starting point. Other design team members as observers should be kept to a minimum, once again to avoid a crowd of observers in the room.

II. During the Session

1. Downplay the fact that it is a pilot session. There is no need to be secretive about the fact. But frequent reference to the session as a pilot can have several negative results. First, participants may feel they are attending an unfinished or imperfect program. Second, participants may concentrate so much on their roles as evaluators that they do not really experience the program. Third, participants sometimes feel it is their duty to find faults in the program just because it is a pilot. It is then hard for them to really participate and get involved in the program.

You may want to simply state that the program is still relatively new and, therefore, open to minor adjustments.

2. Hold daily instructor briefing sessions. These sessions are essential for both instructors and design people. First, you cannot rely on even experienced instructors to automatically know whether the session is going as planned and how to adjust as the session proceeds. This session, therefore, helps instructors adjust their approach as the session progresses. These sessions will also serve as a debriefing for the design people present. Problem areas can be noted, changes to materials can be made, and possible solutions or changes can be documented for future use.

When analyzing problems or considering on-the-spot changes, always use the original program design as your reference point. Changes should only be considered if they are consistent with the original design objectives. Minor changes should be noted for the next session without any adjustment to the current session. The following chapter contains guidelines about when it is necessary to fix a problem on the spot and when it is not.

3. Collect as much data as possible.   You may not be getting all the information you need through formal channels, and there are many informal opportunities to collect information about how the program is going. Take advantage of breaks and meals to talk informally with participants. The next chapter on fixing broken training programs also contains ideas for gathering information and describes clues that may indicate problems early in the program. Collecting this information is part of the observer's job at a pilot program and often has a higher payoff than meeting with instructors or other observers.

III. After the Session

1. Resolve any problems that emerged during the pilot.   The notes taken at the session are invaluable in making decisions about changes afterward. You may also find it helpful to test ideas on change with participants. Most participants welcome this contact as proof of your commitment to quality and your willingness to listen to feedback. If some participants are particularly concerned about certain problems, let them know how those problems are being resolved. Just as after other tests, changes should be made as soon after the pilot session as possible, while the data are fresh.

2. Finalize instructor notes.   These notes should reflect the Design Document, the notes taken at the pilot session, and any changes agreed on after the pilot. They should be completed as soon as possible after the pilot session.

3. Publicize the pilot results.   Obviously this is easiest if the pilot is successful. You should not hesitate to use this success as a source of visibility and publicity for the program. Even if changes are necessary, you can emphasize the positive aspects of the pilot and let people know that you are continuing to perfect the program.

4. Inform design team members of pilot results.   Since all members of the team probably were not present at the pilot, let them know how the session went. You may also want to inform

---

REQUIREMENTS

Materials: All participant and instructor materials; Design Document and Program Specifications for reference; participant background sheets or applications.

Time: The full time needed for the finished program. Additional time will probably be required for reviewing the pilot session and making needed changes.

People: A group of participants appropriate to the program; instructors; at least one member of the design team as observer. Future instructors may attend as participants. One designer team member may attend for the purpose of writing instructor notes.

Budget: Normal costs for a program session including facility, instructor, and materials costs.

Facilities: Normal facilities required by the final program.

---

people who participated in the materials test or in other stages of development.

REMEMBER

The design team may view the pilot session as the final test of the program. But do not delude yourself that the organization sees it in the same way. To the participants and the organization, the pilot session is *the* program, no matter what you may tell them. Therefore, every aspect of the pilot should be as finished and as well executed as possible.

During the pilot session, remain calm and objective. Don't panic and adjust your design every time a problem arises. Look at each problem and ask yourself whether, realistically, it prevents participants from having a productive session. If not, then note the feedback and solution ideas and decide how to solve the problem later when you have perspective on the entire session.

If the session is clearly deteriorating because of the problem, then you may want to explore the situation openly with participants and make necessary changes. These changes may be stopgap measures just to help this session, or they may turn out to be the final changes needed to solve the problem. Remember that when a comprehensive design and development process has been used, most pilot sessions require only minor adjustments, which can be made after the session is over. You often create more confusion by stopping the session to make changes than by continuing and then reviewing needed changes after the session is over.

The project manager or design team representative should prevent other observers from overreacting to problems during the session and particularly from sharing their concerns with the participants when it is not appropriate.

LOOKING AHEAD

You have now completed the design and development process for this program. The program can now be delivered on a regular basis. Materials can be produced and stockpiled for future programs. Any instructor training session can be held and instructor notes distributed.

Of course, the program will evolve slowly as it is used and adapted. Whenever possible, these enrichments should be shared among instructors and even introduced into the instructor notes and the Design Document. Any major future revisions of the program should use the Design Document as a starting point, so that important design considerations are not lost. In this way, the work you have done during the design and development process will continue to serve throughout the life of the program.

11

HOW TO FIX A "BROKEN" TRAINING PROGRAM

A "broken" training program can be anything from a simple exercise with unclear instructions to an entire program that has no relevance for the participants. The fault may lie with a minor timing problem or with a drastic miscalculation of participants' needs. But, whatever part of the program is "broken," the principles for fixing it are the same.

One principle is central to all efforts to fix a training program: *Do not fix what is not really "broken."* This means two things.

First, before taking any action, make sure the program really has a problem. It is natural to search immediately for problems (and solutions) within the program design, especially when that is your area of expertise. But first rule out problems that don't come from the design, such as inadequate instructors, facility problems, poor selection of participants, or a negative climate in the organization. Don't assume, on the basis of one session, that the fault lies with the program itself. If you do, you may spend a lot of time and money solving problems that don't exist.

Second, don't "over-fix" a problem. Don't rewrite an entire role-play just because the observer forms were confusing. Don't re-do an entire simulation just because participants needed more information. Instead, find out *exactly* what is wrong and take the least action possible to fix it. This suggestion is not to minimize work but to disturb the program design as little as possible. Each change made in the program raises the possibility of disturbing the overall design. Of course, you can and should foresee the effect of changes on the overall design and adjust accordingly. But the smaller the change made, the less danger of creating other design problems.

THINGS TO WATCH OUT FOR

Fixing a "broken" training program is often viewed as a crisis situation. There are some common pitfalls that can arise from the sense of confusion and failure that can accompany such a situation.

One pitfall is the panic that may occur on the part of the training professionals when a problem appears. Panic can lead to "over-fixing" the program or to exaggerating the problem. It can also lead to action on the first definition of the problem, which may turn out to be inaccurate. Instead, admit calmly that a problem appears to exist. Focus on fixing the problem, not on affixing blame. Be open to all possible explanations and solutions. Keep in mind that there is a logical process for handling problems and that such problems are a common part of the development process.

Another pitfall is the panic of the sponsor. When that happens, avoid being defensive. But also avoid being over-solicitous. It is tempting, in your attempt to "make up" for the problem, to agree to anything the sponsor wants. But such an approach appears unprofessional and may cause bigger problems later on. You will earn more respect if you emphasize the importance of careful data-gathering and analysis before you jump into action.

Sometimes the sponsor, deciding that "the less said the better," simply wants to forget the whole thing. Try to convince him or her to revise the program. Your credibility will be enhanced, and the organization will get the program it wants. Emphasize that problems are common and that any bad feelings that have been created are almost always erased when an improved program is presented.

Sometimes the sponsor may want to change the whole program, even though you feel strongly that only partial changes are required or that the problem lies outside the program design. In that case, make it clear to the sponsor that you can and will make the program successful, but that the sponsor needs to trust you and your capabilities. Then gather data that support your point of view before letting yourself be forced into a complete redesign of the program.

Sometimes organizations fall into the trap of using their least-valuable resources to fix a program, usually because they feel too much time and money has already been used. But it is precisely on revision projects that first-rate people should be used. Fixing a program requires experience and perspective. It is not the time to allow inexperienced people to try out their skills.

Repair projects sometimes falter because the people involved are too close to the topic to use good judgment. If that is the case, bring in credible experienced people who were not involved before. They can give a refreshing view and may also demonstrate to others your commitment to making the program right.

A dangerous pitfall is when the training people retire to lick their wounds and fix things without further involvement of the sponsor. This may happen because the sponsor retreats or because the project team feels the need to regroup in private. In either case, this approach will only lead to further problems. The sponsor must understand what went wrong and commit to your plan to fix it in order to give you the advice and support you need.

A final pitfall is to postpone any action. This is sometimes tempting if feelings are high or if the work schedule is busy. But such a delay has several negative effects. First, an organization often sees immediate action as decisive and positive, while action taken several months later is seen as "dragging that thing out again." Second, the impressions and notes from the program presentation are not as fresh. Third, the sponsors' commitment to act often declines with time.

Now let's look at exactly how to move ahead.

DEFINING THE PROBLEM

The title of this chapter may be misleading. Often, fixing a program is the easiest part. The most difficult task is correctly diagnosing the problem, discovering what is not working and why.

During the Program

Defining the program begins with being alert to hints of a problem during the actual program presentation. When program developers and instructors are shocked by a negative evaluation at the end of a program, it sometimes means that they were not sensitive to signs of a problem during the program. Below are some clues that may tell you all is not well. This doesn't mean that you should panic if any one of these clues is present. But any one clue should make you sensitive to other signs, which may confirm that all is not well.

1 *Participants don't want to talk about the program.* In response to casual questions about how it's going or about their reaction

to a particular unit, people consistently either change the subject or give very superficial answers. It is normal for participants, returning from exercises or going to breaks, to talk about what has been happening. If they are not talking about it, something may be wrong.

2 *The program developers, instructors, or other non-participants present are not included in social activities or not encouraged to join in.* When participants don't make small talk or try to get to know the non-participants, it may indicate a problem. Of course, there are circumstances when the participants are busy or the non-participants indicate they don't want to interact. But if a reasonable effort is made by the non-participants and there is no encouragement, then something may be wrong.

3 *Participants don't ask for help with activities and don't ask for additional information or ideas.* Obviously, not all participants ask for help. But if you are accessible and no one asks for your help or ideas, there may be something wrong.

4 *Humorous remarks in the classroom never have any connection to class activities or topics.* It is natural for people to make jokes about the things they are discussing and doing. If this doesn't happen, look for other clues.

5 *Participants make more cynical remarks than normal.* Some such remarks are always present, but an experienced training person can sense when they are excessive. Lots of negative references to the organization may indicate a negative climate or specific current events that are worrying people and making them unreceptive to the program.

6 *Participants don't do evening assignments or individual assignments.*

7 *People are late or skip sessions altogether.*

When any or several of these clues are present, it is a good idea to start gathering more information. Take every opportunity to interact with the participants. If people ask about your queries, explain that you are concerned that the program meet their needs and indicate that the program is still being finalized. Probe for details and suggestions for change. But do not promise specific changes until you have the commitment of others involved in presenting the program.

If the problem appears to be a major one, consider asking for formal feedback and suggestions from the participants as a group. Naturally, pausing during the course to gather this kind of information will highlight the fact that problems exist. However, if everyone is already aware that the program is not satisfactory, it is better to acknowledge that fact and indicate your openness to change. If you continue instead to plod through the planned activities, participants can only assume that you do not realize there is a problem or are not interested in fixing it. Either assumption will be damaging to your credibility.

When problems become clear during the course of the program presentation, a decision must be made. Should you make changes on the spot or wait until the whole program has been seen and more information has been gathered?

The determining factor in this situation is usually the magnitude of the problem. For example, if it is apparent that the task force method has been over-used, then it is reasonable to change the next day's exercise to another form. However, if there seems to be a major problem with the content chosen for the program, changes to address that problem will involve the entire program design and should probably be put off until the program is over. But even if the basic problem cannot be addressed on the spot, you may want to make a few interim changes, which will help the current situation but will not necessarily become part of the program's final design.

After the Program

Once the program is over, you can use several methods to gather information about what went wrong. If you gathered information during the program session, you may feel that the problem has already been defined; but you should still explore the causes of the problem later. The initial diagnosis may provide only some of the answers, and may not generate the best possible solution. Remember that defining the problem is the hardest part of fixing a program. Take plenty of time to do it right before you jump into action.

First, if you have the luxury of another presentation of the program before any action has to be taken, then someone should sit in on that session. For that presentation, change any factors, such as the instructors or the facility, that might have caused the problem. This allows you to test whether or not it is the design that is really at fault. During the session, collect as much data as possible and compare that data to what you learned at the previous session. If you attended the previous session, you may choose to have someone else attend this one to lend a new perspective.

Second, use written feedback to gather information. You will probably have program evaluations filled out by participants at the end of the program. These can be useful but may not contain the in-depth questions you now need to ask. Therefore, when you have studied the standard evaluations, you may decide to send out a more detailed reaction form to the participants. If participants are aware that you are considering changing the program, they will probably be glad to provide more information. If you feel participants won't complete the forms, you may decide to do only interviews.

Third, you may choose to do some in-depth interviews with the program participants. In other words, find out how to fix the program from the people who said it was "broken." Interviews allow you to probe more deeply and to follow other avenues of thought introduced by interviewees. They also allow you to gather detailed ideas about how to improve the program. Although participants may not know about training, they are well able to tell you what they would like to have experienced during the program. This may lead you to solutions that otherwise may not have occurred to you. You may also find that their suggestions involve far less change than you might have otherwise undertaken.

In all your data-gathering efforts, remember to focus on exactly what bothered the participants. For example, if a group exercise is described as "a waste of time" by participants, find out whether they (a) didn't like the activity, (b) thought it took too long, (c) didn't feel they took anything concrete away from the exercise, or (d) felt the case materials used were not technically accurate. Correctly inter-preting what they mean by "a waste of time" will make an enormous difference in the action you take.

Remember also to find out how serious a problem is. If you inter-view a participant and ask how he or she felt about a certain exercise, the participant may respond that he or she "didn't like it." But you still don't know whether that dislike for the exercise ruined the pro-gram for that person or whether it was a very minor aspect of the experience. If you find out how serious a problem it was, then you can decide how much attention the problem warrants.

Many training program problems result from some part of the de-sign and development process being left out, done wrong, or done incompletely. Therefore, in analyzing data, you may want to ask yourself questions that will identify what part of the process went wrong. You will need answers to the following questions:

- Was the original need accurately defined?
- Were the objectives appropriate to meet the identified needs?
- Did the program design achieve the established objectives?
- Was the content appropriate to the objectives?
- Were the methodologies appropriate for the participants, for the content, and for the objectives? Was one methodology over-used?
- Were the flow and transitions logical and easy to follow?
- Were the materials of good quality, well written, and interesting?
- Did the materials do what the design intended them to do?
- Was sufficient testing done to catch problems in the materials?
- Were the design and materials tested with the right people (people who could give designers accurate feedback)?
- Were the instructors skilled? prepared? Did they have complete, accurate information?
- Was there good coordination between developers and sponsors? Did the sponsors review the design and materials in depth? Were the sponsors kept up to date? Were conflicts between developers and sponsors resolved effectively? The answers to these questions may not indicate the solution to the problem, but they may suggest changes in the process to avoid future problems.
- Was the group a normal one in terms of receptivity? Did the participants represent an unusual combination of problems, attitudes, or back-home concerns?
- Were the logistics of the program smoothly planned and executed (registration, facilities, equipment, etc.)? Although these factors alone seldom cause a program to fail, they can make other problems seem more serious.

SOLVING THE PROBLEM

Once the problem is defined to your satisfaction, you are ready to decide on a solution. Once again, be aware of over-fixing a problem. Try to identify the simplest possible change that will solve the problem. Then test the idea with those who initially identified the problem. Do this with former participants as well as design and development people and sponsors.

Finding the Solution

Let's examine some of the most common reasons for "broken" seminars and how to fix them.

1 *The original need(s) were not accurately defined.* You will now need to redefine the needs. You may either re-do the Needs Analysis or do one if it was never done. Or you may only need to re-do the analysis of the information gathered. Before starting to re-do any part of the Needs Analysis, decide where the original one went wrong. Did it involve the right people? Were the right questions asked? Did the sponsor unduly influence the interpretation of the results?

2 *The objectives did not meet the needs identified.* This may be the result of hurried or inexperienced people converting the needs to program objectives. Go back to the original needs and repeat the process of establishing objectives. Be sure to involve people who represent all important perspectives.

   The content of the program is usually defined primarily by the objectives. Therefore, if the content is found to be inappropriate, examine and redefine the objectives as described above.

3 *The program activities or methodologies did not fit the program objectives.* In this case, revisit the design and carefully analyze why each activity or methodology was used. Did it contribute to the objectives established, or was that activity or methodology included for other reasons? Those reasons might include personal preference of the designers or sponsors, past successes of other programs, or lack of other known alternatives. Then make changes that will ensure that the activities and methods support the program objectives.

4 *Program activities and methodologies fit the objectives of the program but were inappropriate for the participants.* This bad fit may be due to such factors as preferences of the participants, sophistication of the participants, past experiences with activities and methods, or simple boredom due to over-use of some methodologies. Review the design and ask which activity or methodology is most appropriate in each unit. Then make ap-

propriate changes to the design. These changes will often involve only one or two units of the program.

The type of design problems described above may be due to inexperienced project team members or members who do not accept different methodologies. If this is the case, you may need to bring in additional resources who can bring up new alternatives or address prejudices and misunderstandings. These may be resources within the organization or from outside.

5 *The flow and transitions are not logical.* This often happens when the overall flow of the program was never thought through. Once you sit down and think about the connection between each unit and the overall logic behind the arrangement of units, the trouble spots usually become apparent and can be addressed. If the nature of the problems or their solutions do not become apparent, then you may need to get help from others. This problem often requires changes in the overall program design, since it affects many units as well as the relationship between the units.

6 *The materials were of poor quality, inaccurate, or uninteresting.* In this case, the materials can usually just be rewritten. If the content of the materials is at fault, you may need to consult former participants or experts in the subject matter. If the problem is with interest or writing quality, development people can usually solve the problem.

7 *Materials are themselves well written but do not accomplish what the design meant them to do.* For example, you may have an excellent case study, but it does not bring out the desired learning points. Once again, the solution is to rewrite the materials.

Sometimes the problem is defined either as insufficient testing of the materials or testing with the wrong people. But the result and the solution are the same as described above for poor materials. Better testing would simply have allowed you to correct the materials before the program was presented. This is a valuable lesson but does not alter the way you solve the problem.

8 *The instructor was not adequate.* If the problem was instructor skills, you probably need to change instructors. Even if the instructor can improve his or her skills, the fixing of this program may not be the place to practice. If the instructor was poorly prepared or given insufficient information, then find out what

was missing last time and make sure that he or she now has everything needed. You may also want to work closely with the instructor in preparing for the next session. Sometimes, even if the instructor's skills were not the problem, you may have to change instructors for reasons of appearance and public relations.

9 *Composition of the group.* This may be a one-time problem in which an unfortunate combination of people attended the program. For example, there may have been a large number of people who resisted a recent strategy shift by the organization and therefore encouraged each other to be negative and closed-minded. The group might have been polarized between young fast-trackers and long-time employees, so that energy was spent on bad feelings between those groups rather than on learning. If you believe there was a destructive combination of participants, simply review the participant list for the next session to make sure it doesn't happen again. If the selection process makes a repeat combination likely, consider controlling the selection process or changing it altogether.

10 *Logistics of the program.* Normally, these factors alone do not cause problems. However, they should still be fixed for the next presentation. Sometimes changes in logistics are perceived by others as symbolic actions showing your concern and decisiveness.

Implementing the Solution

Now that you've decided how to fix the problem, it is critical to stop and consider the effect of your solution on the rest of the program. Do the flow and transitions still make sense? Does any new material duplicate other pieces of the program? Have any activities, methodologies, or topics been over-used as a result of the change? Is anything now missing?

Refer back to the Program Specifications, just as you did when you reviewed the original design. Make sure that the specifications are still met. For example, to fix the problem of a boring unit, you may decide to use an interesting new technology. But, upon reviewing the original Program Specifications, you find that your latest decision violates a requirement that no special equipment be required for the program. You now have to decide how to reconcile the two requirements; but it is better to address this conflict now than when the program is implemented.

TESTING THE IMPROVED PROGRAM

You may encounter resistance to testing the changed portions of the program before running it again. Some people may feel that there is no doubt about the problem having been solved. Others may feel that testing the program requires time and money that have already been used up by earlier problems. Sponsors may resist another test for political or public relations reasons. It is important to persevere. You cannot afford to let untested changes spoil a complete presentation of the program again. The organization will probably be tolerant of the need to improve a program. It is important, however, that the changes work well if your credibility is to be restored.

Consider using former participants for the test. They are usually flattered by your desire to respond to their complaints and they understand the problem you have addressed. If you cannot use past participants, be sure that the people selected for the test are favorably disposed to training and to this particular program. Any prejudice or distraction on their part will skew the results of your test.

Obviously, you will want to ensure that instructors, facilities, and other outside factors are not going to cause problems at the test. Such problems would skew the results of the test and make it hard to tell if the initial problem has been solved.

PUBLICIZING THE SUCCESS

Once the program is fixed, be sure the fact is well publicized. Your credibility will be greatly enhanced if people realize you responded to their needs, stood by your work, and knew how to fix the problem.

"Broken" training programs are an inevitable part of a training professional's existence. They can be revised calmly, efficiently, and systematically. They can result in a much stronger program and enhanced credibility for the people involved. And they don't *have* to take ten years off your life!

PART

2

A SURVEY OF MAJOR
TRAINING METHODOLOGIES
AND HOW TO USE THEM

1

TASK FORCE EXERCISE

DESCRIPTION

A *task force exercise* is one in which the participants, divided into small groups of three to eight, work concurrently on an assigned task or tasks, often presenting their results to the assembled class.

PURPOSE

The purpose of this method is to allow participants to work with the content or learning of the unit in a group small enough for everyone to contribute and be involved.

When to Use a Task Force Exercise

A task force exercise can be effective when one or more of the following is true:

1 The objective is

- to test the participants' understanding of a model, concept, or process
- to have participants build on one another's ideas
- to generate a plan or other specific outcome to be used by participants or others in the real work situation
- to give participants confidence in their ability to do the same task back on the job
- to have participants work collaboratively
- to have participants practice analytical skills

- to acknowledge and tap participants' competence, knowledge, and experience

2 The subject is

- one that requires or uses a specific process or set of guidelines
- one that requires creative or collaborative thinking
- one that requires information that only some participants have

3 The group is

- diverse in experience and level of knowledge
- able to discuss and analyze in a group setting
- knowledgeable about the topic or task in question
- in need of feeling a sense of accomplishment
- in need of feedback about how they work as a group

How a Task Force Exercise Typically Works

1 The instructor introduces the exercise. (See Chapter 9 for guidelines on giving instructions.)
2 Participants work in small groups to complete the task within a specified time period.
3 Each group presents its task force results to the entire class, allowing time for comments and questions from other participants. (If desired, instructor can provide feedback or give awards for the best group work.)
4 Instructor summarizes the exercise in one of several ways, including

- reviewing the process used
- pointing out common points in presentations
- summarizing the process used in the small groups
- summarizing obstacles the groups encountered
- giving guidelines for future work

The exact content of the summary will depend on the subject and objectives of the task force, but some form of closure should be provided.

Variations on Task Force Exercises

1 Instructor may give extensive help to groups or none at all, depending on the exercise objectives. For example, if the objective is to give participants a positive experience, the instructor will give enough help to ensure that the group works well. If the objective is to show participants how tricky this task can be, then the instructor will want to leave them alone to experience those typical difficulties.

2 Presentation of group results is usually given orally soon after the group work is completed. But it may also be given in written form or in oral form, which is later typed and distributed to participants. A presentation may not be included in the design or may be delayed if required by the design.

Process for Developing a Task Force Exercise

1 Decide

- what tasks you want the group to perform
- what results you want the group to produce and the format in which they should be presented, if any
- how results will be used. (For example, class presentations, post-program use by participants, basis for later exercise, organizational use)
- what information participants need to perform task
- how the needed information will be provided. (For example, pre-reading, attachments to the exercise instructions, experts available)
- logistics of how exercise will work. (For example, timing, forming groups, where they will work, equipment)
- whether any specialized roles — leader, spokesperson, observer, facilitator — should be assigned or selected by the group and, if so, how

2 Finalize the list of materials needed (for example, exercise instructions, sample of results needed, background information, debrief or observation instructions).

3 Draft all materials needed.

Common Reasons for Ineffective Task Force Exercises

1 Task to be performed is

- not clear to participants
- too complex or lengthy for time allowed
- too easy, either for time allowed or for skill or knowledge of participants

2 The participants react to highly competitive environment by concentrating on "beating the other guys" rather than on doing a good job.

3 The standards for exercise results are

- not clear
- not high enough to be challenging

4 The exercise

- does not provide enough information in its instructions for participants to do the task
- has unclear instructions and/or the instructor is not available to clear up the confusion
- duplicates previous program activities in subject or form

2

CASE DISCUSSION

DESCRIPTION

A *case discussion* uses a *case study* — a description of a situation in writing, on audio tape, or on video tape — which the participants study and then discuss, guided by the questions and probing of the instructor. A typical case discussion focuses on the issues involved in the situation, what action should be taken or what lessons can be learned, and how to handle or avoid such situations in the future.

PURPOSE

This method allows participants to discover certain learning points themselves rather than simply receiving them from the instructor. Case discussions attempt to teach people, or allow people to practice using, the thought processes needed to analyze a real situation and to identify possible actions. This method is *not* designed to teach people the "right" solution for a given situation.

When to Use a Case Study

A case study can be effective when one or more of the following is true:

1 The objective is

- to teach awareness rather than specific skills
- to teach analysis skills rather than the "right" answer

- to simulate a real-life situation in limited time with limited resources
- to encourage people to participate
- to demonstrate that the program content is not just conceptual, but applies to the real world
- to give participants a chance to air their views or vent their emotions
- to make participants more confident about the validity of their views and their ability to analyze situations and come up with solutions
- to test participants' understanding of concepts, approaches, and issues

2 The subject is

- complex and many-sided
- not one that lends itself to any one answer

3 The group is

- sophisticated, able to organize and deal with large amounts of information
- skilled at analysis
- large (ten to thirty participants) and individual participation is desirable
- confident and articulate enough to express opinions, to challenge, and to reinforce one another
- opinionated or emotional and needs a chance to air their views or emotions

How a Case Discussion Typically Works

1 The instructor introduces the case and guides the participants to the correct focus.
2 Participants read and analyze the case in preparation for discussion.
3 Instructor starts and guides the participants' discussion, asking questions, probing, and summarizing.
4 Instructor may use flipcharts or blackboard to document the flow of discussion.

5 Instructor summarizes the learning points or issues brought out by the case.
6 If the case will be used in the next activity, instructor connects the discussion to that activity.

Types of Case Studies

1 A *classic case study* is used to generate discussion about what is happening, right or wrong, in a situation, how the situation got that way, and how to fix or avoid a similar situation.
2 A so-called "Gateway" case study is used to simulate thinking, create a need to learn, or introduce a role-play or other exercise.
3 A *vignette,* often called a "minicase," is a simple short case study, which usually focuses on choices of action or tests the participants' use of new knowledge.
4 A *positive example* case, illustrating the right way to do something, is not always useful, because it is so one-sided that it does not generate discussion.

Common Formats for Case Studies

Some common formats for case studies include the following:

- retrospective (flashbacks)
- mixture of background and dialogue (for example, between subordinate and manager or two subordinates)
- same situation described from several points of view
- pure narrative or analysis, usually lengthy, used in more academic settings such as business schools

Process for Developing a Case Study

1 Specify learning points and issues to bring out.
2 Determine the type of case study and decide what situation could illustrate desired learning points, considering the following factors:

- should it be a real situation, an invented one, or a combination
- which situation is most relevant or familiar to participants
- not too technical or recognizable, to prevent participants from getting side-tracked (their industry vs. unrelated one)
- is situation too political to get facts or objective views

3 Devise the particulars of the case situation, such as characters and time format.

4 Outline possible characters and action, either before or after interviews. If needed, develop a pro/con list for each view you want brought out, so you can be sure those points are represented in the case.

5 Interview to obtain information needed. You will need appropriate events and a balance of information supporting each view you want discussed.

6 Write the case.

7 Check draft against pro/con graphs or outlines created earlier.

Common Reasons for Ineffective Case Discussions

The case study

- lacks subtlety (class is told issues or points, rather than being allowed to discover them on their own)
- does not reflect reality

  - characters are not real, merely caricatures
  - language is stilted and unrealistic
  - events are too black and white

- gives unneeded information or is too technical
- does not leave people where you want them. For example, you might want participants to be

  - opinionated (vs. no opinion)
  - outraged (vs. don't care)
  - reminded of own job (vs. feeling people are unreal)
  - wanting to discuss (vs. not caring)

- does not contain information that allows several views to come out in the discussion
- uses material that is too "close to home" (leads participants to be too invested in the content to discuss it objectively)
- contains inaccurate information

3

SIMULATIONS AND GAMES

DESCRIPTIONS

A *game* is a formalized activity, usually unrelated to the business environment. The participants attempt to meet a defined objective within the limitations imposed by a set of rules, which determine the game's activities and termination.

A *simulation* represents a real-life business situation, but duplicates the components of the situation and the relationship between the components in such a way that they can be manipulated by the participants within the time frame of the seminar.

PURPOSE

A simulation or game recreates a process, event, or set of circumstances, usually complex, so that participants can experience and manipulate the situation without risk and then analyze what happened.

When to Use a Simulation or a Game

A game or simulation can be effective when one or more of the following is true:

1 The objective is

- to integrate and apply a complex set of skills
- to provide realistic job-related experiences
- to elicit participants' natural tendencies and provide feedback on those tendencies

- to elicit full group participation

2 The subject is

- a sensitive or ambiguous topic, such as trust, power, or cooperation
- a topic that people are reluctant or unable to discuss in a traditional way

3 The group is

- in need of an activity that generates interest and energy
- tending to give "the right answers" in a discussion when they behave differently in real life

How a Simulation or Game Typically Works

1 The instructor introduces the exercise. (See Chapter 9 for guidelines on giving instructions.)
2 The participants prepare by studying the rules, determining strategy, determining their first move, and so on.
3 If necessary, a trial run is held to test understanding.
4 A simulation or game may have several rounds, divided by

- feedback and/or
- new planning and/or
- introduction of new information or rules

5 The results of the game or simulation are tabulated and announced to the participants, if appropriate.
6 The instructor leads a debriefing session, including feedback and discussion of what has gone on in the exercise, and provides an appropriate summary.

Variables in a Simulation or Game

In a simulation or game, the following elements can be varied:

- degree of structure
- degree to which roles are identified or assigned
- amount of instructor manipulation of events during the exercise

- mechanism and frequency of feedback, from debrief to written forms to computer feedback
- degree of similarity to the participants' real job situation

Process for Developing Simulations and Games

1 Decide

  - the learning points for the exercise
  - what issues or emotions you want to bring out
  - what situation can bring out those issues or emotions and whether situation should be job related or not
  - what defined roles will be needed
  - what are the desirable outcomes of the exercise
  - what rules and structure will produce the desired outcome

2 Test the possible options participants will have, given the structure chosen. Define the actions, outcomes, and conflicts that will probably result from each option.
3 Work out the logistics of the exercise, including timing and how the debriefing and feedback will take place.
4 Finalize the list of materials needed.
5 Do any interviews necessary to gather background information.
6 Draft all materials needed.

Common Reasons for Ineffective Simulations or Games

The game or simulation

- is too complex — every element should have a purpose
- is not realistic (if supposed to be)
- is not relevant or interesting to participants
- does not have enough options to make the experience interesting
- has an optimal path so clear or simple that exercise is not challenging
- over-emphasizes winning, so the competitive aspects overwhelm other elements
- lacks clarity
- has a structure that does not bring out the issues and behaviors to be examined

- has a structure in which behavior needed to "win" is not behavior you want to encourage or reinforce
- does not include sufficient discussion and exploration of what happened

ROLE-PLAY EXERCISE

DESCRIPTION

A *role-play exercise* is one in which participants simulate a real or hypothetical interactive situation. It is usually followed by discussion and analysis, to determine how the interaction felt, what happened, and why. Participants can receive feedback on their actions during the role-play.

PURPOSE

Role-plays allow participants to experience how a given interaction may feel or look or sound, using either the participants' customary approach or a new approach or skill. This method also gives participants an opportunity to practice this new approach or skill and provides them with feedback on their behavior in the interaction.

When to Use a Role-Play Exercise

A role-play exercise can be effective when one or more of the following is true:

1 The objective is

- to allow participants to practice skills needed in a given situation
- to have participants learn what the interactive situation feels like
- to assess the participants' behavior in an interactive situation

111

- to allow participants to practice observational skills
- to build participants' confidence in their ability to handle a given situation
- to identify what behavior is effective and ineffective in a given situation

2 The subject is

- more complex than it seems, so that participants need to experience it
- hard to understand through only discussion and analysis

3 The group is

- from different backgrounds or jobs, so they need a common experience as a basis for discussion
- in need of a real-world exercise after a lot of conceptual material
- lacking confidence about handling this type of situation
- overconfident so that they need to see their need for improvement

How a Role-Play Exercise Typically Works

1 The instructor introduces the exercise. (See Chapter 9 for guidelines on giving instructions.)
2 Participants prepare for the role-plays, either alone or in groups.
3 The class enacts the role-plays, either in small groups or as a class. (See *Common Types of Role-Plays*.)
4 Role-play is discussed and feedback given as appropriate, either in small groups or in class. Discussion may take place first in small groups, then in class.
5 The learning points of the exercise are summarized, either by the instructor or through group presentations.

Common Learning Models for Role-Plays

1 Discovery model: Participants handle the situation whatever way they wish, then analyze what happened and draw conclusions for handling future situations.
2 Practice model: Participants are given way(s) to handle the sit-

uation, then practice handling the situation in that way and receive feedback on how well they did.

Common Types of Role-Plays

1 Small groups:

- one situation enacted once (single)
- one situation enacted several times with role rotation (repeat)
- several situations, each enacted once with roles rotated for each situation (sometimes called round robin)

2 Fishbowl: One or more groups role-playing in front of the rest of the class. It can use the same situation for all groups or different ones for each group.

Variables in Role-Plays

1 Source of situation:

- pre-determined, with a written description
- a real-life situation of the participant, with an oral or written description prepared by the participant before or during the program (often called write-your-own role-play)
- selected from real life by the group

2 Amount of preparation time and additional role information given:

- no additional information; no preparation
- written instructions outlining basic facts, but no point of view; short preparation period
- detailed instructions including objectives, point of view, and additional facts; formal preparation period

3 Reason for stopping during role-play:

- to allow participants to get help or start over
- to bring in new players, either spontaneously or according to plan

- to analyze, either verbally or in writing
- to ask for reactions or feedback
- to reverse roles

4 Mechanism for giving feedback:

- written rating forms
- video tape or audio tape (watched/listened to by participant and others or participant alone)
- structured discussion of class or small group
- unstructured discussion of class or small group
- presentation by the instructor
- any combination of the above

5 Source of feedback:

- participant(s) assigned as observer(s)
- other role players (from memory or video of session)
- entire class as observers
- instructor
- participant who played role (through self-rating or watching video of session)

Materials Usually Needed for Role-Plays

The following materials are usually needed for role-plays:

- general instructions (introduction, payoff, role structure, process, timing, etc.)
- individual role instructions
- observer instructions, if observer used, including observation forms
- written rating forms, if used
- written guidelines for post–role-play discussion, if appropriate

Process for Developing a Role-Play Exercise

1 Decide

- the learning model and structure of the role-play
- what issues the role-play should raise or investigate

- what conflict or different views are involved
- what situation and characters would typically be involved when these issues arise
- what point of view each character might take (outline these to be sure the appropriate points are known to each character)
- how much time is needed for preparation, role-playing, and debrief
- what kind of feedback will be given and how
- how results will be discussed and summarized

2 Finalize list of materials needed.
3 Interview as required to collect background or anecdotal information.
4 Draft all materials needed.
5 Test that characters are given all the information they would logically have in a real situation and that all the information is consistent.

Common Reasons for Ineffective Role-Plays

1 The situation

- is not clearly outlined
- involves no conflict or differences (might be of loyalties, priorities, perceptions, backgrounds, moods, or personalities)
- does not contain a solution within the power of the people in the role-play
- is too complex, so that players get lost

2 The structure is not clear with regard to process, timing, role rotation, or end results.
3 The roles

- are so locked in that no win is possible
- are so locked in that players have no freedom to act or use skills, thus allowing players to abdicate responsibility
- create no pressure to resolve the issues
- are not clear
- contain confusing, incomplete, conflicting or overly technical information

4 The debrief

- process used to discuss role-play is not clear or does not respect sensitivities of participants
- does not force participants to deal with what has happened
- calls for feedback that is irrelevant to participants
- calls for feedback on points that were not possible to demonstrate or not observable during the role-play

5

GROUP DISCUSSION

DESCRIPTION

A *group discussion* is a planned opportunity for participants to freely exchange ideas or opinions in the large group or in sub-groups. Participants are made aware of the parameters of the group discussion. The instructor is responsible for encouraging discussion through questions and probing, then drawing together the ideas and opinions generated and providing closure for the discussion.

PURPOSE

Group discussions enable participants to bring out and exchange various ideas on the subject at hand. They may serve as a "warm up" for an exercise, a summary of an activity, or a stand-alone activity.

When to Use a Group Discussion

A group discussion can be effective when one or more of the following are true:

1 The objective is

- to obtain a variety of opinions
- to generate new or additional ideas
- to draw upon a variety of experiences
- to encourage group interaction
- to have the group apply concepts to their job
- to create synergy

- to build group esteem
- to let the group solve a problem
- to let the group create a plan of action
- to test if the group understands or buys into the discussion topic

2 The subject is

- one in which there is a lot of interest
- one that is not normally discussed
- one about which people have many facts or opinions to share
- one that is related to their experience or existence
- one that is misunderstood or creates misunderstanding

3 The group is

- made up of individuals who feel they hold the only possible view
- more knowledgeable on the topic than the instructor
- in need of reflecting on their opinions
- in need of an opportunity to vent their opinions
- not getting along and differences need surfacing

How a Group Discussion Typically Works

1 Instructor introduces the exercise by explaining the subject and purpose of the discussion
2 Instructor leads group in discussion of topic, using good group discussion skills to get as many participants involved as possible.
3 Instructor may use flipcharts or blackboard to document flow of discussion.
4 Instructor summarizes discussion, reminding participants of main points that emerged and conclusion reached, if any.

Variations on Group Discussion

1 Discussion can be leaderless or led by a participant instead of the instructor.
2 Discussion can be documented on flipcharts or by someone taking notes.
3 Participants may participate spontaneously or prepare before-

hand. In the latter case, discussion sometimes begins with each participant or small-group representative giving his or her opinion or findings on the topic.

4 Leader may start the exercise with a short presentation to provide a framework for the discussion.

5 Discussion can be only for the purpose of discussing the subject, or it can have a specific end result, such as a plan, process, recommendations, and so on.

Process for Preparing for a Group Discussion

1 Decide

- what subject and issues you want group to discuss
- what end result you want discussion to produce
- how discussion will be opened
- pre-work, if any, to prepare participants for discussion
- additional questions or topics you will use to encourage and guide discussion

2 Prepare any pre-work material required.

Common Reasons for Ineffective Group Discussions

1 The discussion leader

- does not make clear the purpose or subject of the discussion
- is not skilled in leading discussions:

  - overcontrols or undercontrols
  - allows one or more group members to dominate the discussion
  - ridicules or puts down participants
  - does not use good questions

2 The discussion

- wanders, does not stay on one topic
- continues too long
- is on a subject that is not relevant or interesting to participants

3 The participants

- feel constrained from expressing their opinion (might be because of politics, the sensitivity of the subject, fear of ridicule, ignorance of the purpose, or lack of background and experience in the subject)
- think discussion is only a "token" and that the leader is not really interested in their comments

6

INDIVIDUAL EXERCISES

DESCRIPTION

An *individual exercise* is one in which each participant works independently, usually to transfer the content or learning points of the program to his or her own situation.

PURPOSE

This method allows participants to apply the program's learning points to their own situation in order to test their understanding or to see how that learning applies to their personal situation.

When to Use an Individual Exercise

An individual exercise can be effective when one or more of the following is true:

1 The objective is

- to make participants aware of how the program's learning is relevant to their job situations
- to have participants prepare to use the program's learning back on the job
- to test the participants' understanding of the content of the program
- to encourage in-depth planning for future action on the job
- to build participants' commitment to do things differently back on the job

- to show participants where they need more knowledge or skills with relation to the program's subject areas

2 The subject is

- one that allows participants to be introspective
- one that involves information unique to each individual (i.e., real-life situation, personal problems, feedback)
- one that might be viewed as threatening, confidential, or sensitive

3 The group is

- made up of people with very different jobs, so that their real-life situations vary
- in need of thinking time
- in need of a change of pace from group activities and discussions
- starting to think back to their real-life situations (i.e., near the end of the program)

How an Individual Exercise Typically Works

1 Instructor introduces the exercise and stresses the responsibility of each participant to concentrate on the task. (See Chapter 9 for guidelines on giving instructions.)
2 Participants work individually while instructor maintains a good working atmosphere and is available for help if appropriate.
3 Where specified by the design, participants share their conclusions or results with others, either in small groups or with the class (often called a reality-test).
4 Instructor addresses any final questions and summarizes how the results of the exercise can be used.

Variations on an Individual Exercise

1 Often individuals will be asked to share their results or reactions later in the program. In that case, such expectations should be clearly explained before the individual work is done.
2 Sometimes an individual exercise requires information or documents from the participant's real job situation. If this is the

case, participants must be warned to bring such information with them to the program.

Process for Developing an Individual Exercise

1 Decide

- what is the task the individual will do
- why the results will benefit the individual and how the results will be used
- what process or written structure will help the participant to do the task (i.e., questions, blanks to fill in, suggested format, steps to follow)
- whether participants will share any part of the exercise with others after the exercise
- what written materials are needed (i.e., instructions, planning format, questions)

2 Draft all needed materials.

Common Reasons for Ineffective Individual Exercises

1 The task

- is vague in nature and no structure or guidelines are provided to help
- is not clearly explained
- is not relevant to participants, or its relevance is not explained in introduction
- does not have a clear payoff to the participant
- is too difficult to do in the time allowed

2 The atmosphere is not quiet and task oriented enough to allow people to work effectively.
3 The follow-up

- involves sharing which makes people uncomfortable because of confidentiality, politics, or other factors
- involves sharing of results for which participants are not prepared because it was not explained before the exercise.

7

PRESENTATION/LECTURETTE

DESCRIPTION

A *presentation/lecturette* is a structured, one-way communication from the presenter/lecturer to the audience. While the audience may ask questions, interactive participation is limited. Frequently, visual aids are used to support the material presented.

PURPOSE

Presentations or lecturettes convey information (usually important new knowledge, views, or approaches) to the participants in a situation where interaction or discussion is not wanted or not possible.

When to Use a Presentation/Lecturette

A presentation/lecturette can be effective when one or more of the following is true:

1 The objective is

- to establish the speaker's credibility
- to communicate the speaker's expertise
- to impart information quickly
- to impart the same amount and quality of information to a number of groups
- to maintain control over the audience
- to set the standard or tone for a program
- to set up an exercise clearly

- to model a presentation/lecturette
- to introduce a new area of content

2 The subject is

- conceptual
- factual
- historical
- theoretical
- new to the audience

3 The group is

- not very knowledgeable or opinionated about the subject being discussed
- large
- receptive to the information
- aware of the need for the speaker to impart his or her expertise

Process for Developing a Presentation/Lecturette

1 Decide

- what you want the participants to know or do at the end of the presentation/lecturette (for example, be aware of new concept, have necessary background for exercise, be motivated to learn more)
- what the participants already know or feel about the topic
- how long the presentation/lecturette needs to be to cover the information (the shorter the better)
- on a maximum of three to four main points, regardless of presentation length
- what supporting material will be effective under each main point
- where visual aids are required to explain or clarify the verbal presentation
- how to introduce presentation/lecturette in a way that makes participants want to listen
- how to conclude presentation/lecturette by summarizing content and importance of material

- if an interactive portion would make a contribution to the group's learning

2 Draft the written copy or outline.
3 Try the presentation/lecturette on someone to test relevance and presence of unneeded material.
4 Revise and finalize presentation/lecturette material.

Common Reasons for Ineffective Presentations/ Lecturettes

1 The presentation/lecturette

- is used when a more interactive learning method is really needed
- is longer than needed (in a training program, should be as short as possible, used only when no other method is usable)
- includes interactive portions only as "tokens," without real need or use for the participants' contribution

2 The presenter/lecturer

- presents information that is irrelevant or of no use to the participants
- over-uses visual aids, so presentation becomes only a reading of the aids
- does not make clear to participants how they can use the information or why it is being presented
- does not link the presentation to other activities or content of the program

8

BEHAVIOR MODELING

DESCRIPTION

In *behavior modeling,* participants are given a step-by-step model for handling a given interaction. Then a demonstration of the steps is provided, usually on video. The participants practice using the steps. Afterward they receive feedback about where they have used the model effectively and where they need to improve.

PURPOSE

Behavior modeling gives participants a specific, proven way to deal with an interactive situation and an opportunity to practice new behavior, so they feel confident in their ability to handle a situation.

When to Use Behavior Modeling

Behavior modeling can be effective when one or more of the following is true:

1 The objective is

- to develop skill proficiency more than intellectual understanding
- to provide a specific sequence of steps for participants to follow
- to get participants to follow a prescribed pattern, or to limit the number of ways a situation is handled

2 The subject is

- one that requires a step-by-step sequence of activities
- one that can be reduced to a consistently appropriate set of steps
- one that is simple conceptually but difficult to execute
- one that involves interaction with others

3 The group is

- too busy in their jobs to analyze and prepare each situation
- demonstrating a higher opinion of their skill level than is accurate
- underestimating how difficult the task is
- lacking in confidence and thus in need of specific guidance and positive feedback

How Behavior Modeling Typically Works

1 The instructor presents the model steps that have been established.
2 A demonstration is shown, usually on video, of the steps being used in a typical situation.
3 Participants analyze how the model was used.
4 Participants practice the model.
5 Feedback is given to each participant about the way he or she used the model.

Variables in Behavior Modeling

In behavior modeling, the following elements can be varied:

- number of practice opportunities
- difficulty of practice opportunities (they can get progressively harder)
- situation of practice opportunities (may involve a standard situation, a situation from the participant's workplace, or a combination of the two)
- mode of feedback after practice (for example, may be from instructor or peers, in writing or verbal)
- use of action plans or contracts for handling the situation back on the job

- whether demonstration "models" use real managers or actors
- whether "models" use specific settings and subjects or generic, neutral ones

Process for Developing Behavior Modeling

1 Decide

  - on the essential steps required in this interaction
  - whether any frequent optional steps should be mentioned
  - the exact wording of the steps

2 Test

  - the written steps for clarity
  - the steps with several typical situations and see if they are widely applicable

3 Decide whether the video model should use actors and generic situations or real people and situations.
4 Do any interviews necessary to gather information for the video model.
5 Write script for video model and test with others to eliminate any possible negative elements or interpretations.
6 Decide

  - type of practice, feedback, and action planning to be used
  - logistics and timing

7 Finalize list of materials needed.
8 Draft any instructions, feedback forms, or other materials needed, in addition to the script.
9 Produce video tape model.

Common Reasons for Ineffective Behavior Modeling

1 The video model

  - is unclear, confusing, or does not effectively represent the desired behavior
  - uses poor actors or production values
  - is so realistic it distracts participants

- is negative or mixed rather than positive
- uses a situation or characters that are not believable

2 The steps defined for the model

- are unclear, vague, or not behavior oriented
- are too numerous for participants to remember
- include too many optional steps or choices

3 The interaction chosen is not relevant to participants, so they have no motivation to be attentive.
4 The interaction chosen is so complex and variable that it is inappropriate for behavior modeling.
5 Participants do not get helpful feedback on their skills, because

- they have not been instructed on how to give positive feedback
- the feedback provided is too vague, badly timed, or nonexistent
- the first (or only) practice is too hard for participants to apply the model

NOTE: Negative models, though sometimes used for impact, are not generally used in behavior modeling. Negative models might be used with other methodologies to dramatize the impact of negative action or to illustrate some common pitfalls in an interaction.

GUIDELINES FOR EXERCISE INSTRUCTIONS

PURPOSE

Written exercise instructions are given

- to present to the participants the information they need to participate in an activity
- for participants to use as a reference point during an activity
- to guide an exercise in the direction intended by the program design
- to ensure consistency in exercise process and results

Steps to Follow in Giving Exercise Directions

1 Introduce the exercise by telling the participants why they are taking part in the activity and how it will benefit them.
2 Give the participants a broad view of what the exercise is about.
3 Direct the participants to read the exercise instructions.
4 Explain how the exercise will work step by step, using a flipchart as necessary.
5 Explain timing, using a flipchart to clarify.
6 Check for participants' understanding.
7 Make assignments regarding tasks, roles, or places to work. Illustrate with flipchart and check for clarity.
8 Clarify by walking through examples of how exercise will work. Ask for questions. Test for understanding.

Common Reasons for Ineffective Instructions

1 Participants are not given an overview of the exercise, so they don't understand how the parts fit together.
2 Participants are not told the payoff of the exercise, so they are not motivated to participate.
3 Information is left out or knowledge is assumed.
4 There are no written instructions when the complexity of the exercise requires them.
5 Different assignments or parts of the activity are not clearly divided or differentiated.
6 Rambling language or a confusing format is used in the written instructions.
7 There are no warnings about common pitfalls (such as running out of time, the importance of the spokesperson, the need for flipcharts, common errors, and so on).

10

DEVELOPING VIDEO FOR TRAINING PROGRAMS

When Is Video Appropriate?

There are many valid reasons for using video in a training program. However, people often include video without ever considering whether video is the right medium for their objectives, their audience, or the content of the training program. Below are some good reasons for using video.

1 *When you want to get the audience's attention.* You want to wake them up, change the pace, introduce some fantasy or fun. Because people are used to television being fun, they look forward to video. The video may or may not help the learning, but that is a different objective. For now, your objective is to get and keep people's interest, and video will do it.

2 *When you need to demonstrate subtle interpersonal points like empathy or enthusiasm.* Video can demonstrate these things well. It can also help people understand the effect of such actions on others. These are usually points that cannot be demonstrated as well in print, because they depend on expression and tone.

3 *When the content is highly conceptual.* These are situations in which "a picture is worth a thousand words." Video can show a complex artistic or architectural form, a physical process hard to imagine in your mind, or a futuristic idea. It can also allow us to view from several spatial perspectives.

4 *When you want to produce an intense experience that will im-*

press people or get them involved. You might show a highly negative experience or a hard-hitting event to get the strong reaction needed for some type of discussion, commitment, or feedback.

5 *When you want to make people receptive.* Because people trust the medium of TV to be entertaining, they may better absorb a subject they normally tune out, such as company hiring policy.

6 *When you want the message to be seen as important.* The company president could put out a memo about the importance of performance appraisal, for example. But if he or she is seen talking about the subject and then going to the trouble of making a video tape on it, people will perceive the message to be more significant.

7 *When you need to deliver a consistent message.* This is often the case with a message that is sensitive and that must be presented in just the right way. Information presented on a video tape is presented in exactly the same manner every time. It will not be skewed, however subtly, by the presenter's personal view, mood, energy level, and so forth.

8 *When you need people to absorb information quickly.* Because video presentations enter the brain by two senses instead of one, information tends to be absorbed faster.

9 *When people need to receive information at various times.* A video tape can be used at the time people can or need to watch it. Groups can watch it when they are at the right place in their group task. Individuals can watch a pre-work or follow-up tape at their own pace.

Not unexpectedly, there is a flip side to the many good uses of video tape. There are some conditions under which video is *not* a good choice.

1 *Don't use video when print can be more intense and detailed.* This includes learning situations in which the content covers a lot of facts and technical details and people need to refer back to them. It also includes case studies in which details of background and statistics will strengthen the case and make the discussion richer.

2 *Don't use video when you want participants to interpret.* Case studies are usually designed to bring out various points of view.

That often happens best when participants are left to imagine what someone looks like, how a remark was delivered, or the tone of a meeting. It is hard to have different interpretations when everything is spelled out on the screen.

3 *Don't use video when the presentation of material needs to be customized.* Video leaves no room for the presenter to adapt the content to the people in the audience; that is, to their mood, their educational level, their previous knowledge, their concerns, or their experiences so far in the training program.

4 *Don't use video simply because it is there.* There are many pressures to use video, including investment in the equipment, the prejudice of management, or a desire to appear modern and state-of-the-art. If these pressures are strong enough, you will use video. But you should recognize the real reason for your motivation and take steps to be sure the video does not compromise the learning in the training program.

How Do You Develop a Training Program Video?

Once you decide to use video in your training program, you will need to go through the following steps.

1 *Make key decisions.* These will help you answer questions the producer will ask you later. They will also help you evaluate later whether you are getting what you want and need. You must decide:

- how the video will be used in the training program (when, relation to other media, etc.)
- who the audience is (age, education, jobs, probable reaction to video, etc.)
- what your objective is (to give information, to motivate, to create a learning exercise)
- what the content of the video is (what information must be covered)
- what the practical considerations are (budget, equipment available, etc.)

2 *Choose the producer.* The producer, also known as communications consultant or producer/director, is your most critical choice in making a video. You should choose the producer your-

self rather than engage an organization to find one for you. Remember, it is the *person* you are choosing, whether he or she is independent or part of a production house. You must feel comfortable with your choice and confident in his or her capabilities. You should not feel reluctant to question or disagree with the producer. Only through an ongoing equal exchange between you and the person you choose will you end up with the video you want and need.

When choosing the producer, be sure he or she has done this kind of work before. A demonstration tape can look very impressive. But if your video is of an entirely different type, his or her demo tape means little.

Be sure to check on the producer's reputation. Don't hesitate to call references. Ask about dependability, flexibility, technical knowledge, and willingness to work out problems.

It is not unusual to talk to three or more producers. They should not be upset that you are talking to others. In fact, their reaction to the competition may give you a clue to their ethics.

Remember that a producer must be a good businessperson. Most training videos don't use state-of-the-art technology or treatments. Therefore you don't need to work with a disorganized, difficult producer who is a poor manager just because he or she is on the leading edge in terms of creativity.

In your initial meeting with the producer, he or she should ask you about the items listed under number 1 above. He or she should probe carefully for your objectives and your concerns. If the producer wants to give you a fixed price proposal after thirty minutes, he or she has not really given your project the thought it deserves.

3 *Review the producer's proposal.* Insist on a fixed price proposal. This may not be possible before the treatment, or even the script, has been developed. If so, the producer is doing this early work on speculation, hoping to get the work. Of course a fixed price will apply only if *you* do not expand the scope. Any unusual overruns are usually negotiated. Be flexible and willing to talk. But remember that you are not obligated to accept additional expenses unless you caused them (i.e., you change your mind on music, you want to change actors, your boss decides to change the date of the shoot at the last minute).

The proposal should also tell you who the key people on the

project will be (producer, director, scriptwriter). It should clearly spell out the number of production days. If asked, the producer should be willing to break the cost down into such categories as talent (the actors), studio costs, editing costs, and so on. The normal profit margin for this type of project should range between 25 and 45 percent, depending on the project and how much the producer wants your business, either now or for the future.

4 *Decide on scenario and format.* The scenario is the way in which the subject will be treated in the video. For example, you might treat the subject of discipline by following one case from beginning to end in a series of scenes. Or you might do a series of quick remarks made by people who have been disciplined. The treatment will depend on your objectives, your audience, your content, and your budget. The format is a function of the scenario. It describes the approach — for example, dramatic, documentary, talk show — and whether the video will be a studio shoot or a location shoot.

The scenario and format may be developed by the producer, who then submits several ideas or variations to you. Or you may develop the scenario working together, usually with the writer present as well. Sometimes writers prepare the scenario working alone. But this does not usually produce as good a product.

Treatment usually refers to a two- or three-page document, which describes the scenario and format but does not include a script.

5 *Write the script.* Normally, this happens after the scenario has been prepared and approved. If you have a script already prepared when you hire the producer, be open to changes or even to starting over again. The producer understands video's potential and constraints much better than you do. He or she and the writer, also experienced with video, may come up with a much better idea or variation on your script.

To start the script-writing process, tell the writer the points you want to make and the order in which you want to make them and provide any supporting documentation that is appropriate. If you feel it is too difficult to pass on all the information, you may even write a rough script and let the producer and writer "video-ize" it for you.

Sometimes the final budget is not submitted until this stage. If so, the producer is actually taking a risk by doing the work up to now.

When you receive the script, it may even include a series of sketches of the scenes to be included, called a storyboard. These storyboards can be quite elaborate, but remember that all such documents cost money to produce and that cost will be passed on to you. Normally you will receive the script in a split-page format, with the actual script on the right-hand side under "Audio." On the left-hand side under "Video" will be the details about camera work, sets, actors, and so on. At this time, you will be concerned primarily with the audio section.

You will want to check the script for accuracy, correct sequence, completeness of information, and any questions of tone, complexity, and so on. You will also be asked to get any necessary approval from within your own organization. Usually a rough draft and a final draft are produced. Any additional drafts may involve an extra charge.

6 *Do pre-production work.* During this period, the producer will be lining up the actors, locations or sets, graphics, and music if needed, plus crew members and studio facilities. All but the last two should be approved by you as the client, although the degree to which you want approval rights will depend on the confidence you have in the producer. Remember, these are your decisions, but use the expertise available to make informed decisions.

7 *Shoot the video.* If pre-production has been well executed, then the video shoot should be smooth and even fun. The client should always attend the shoot, even though his or her presence may sometimes slow things down. The producer must take time to explain how things work. The client may want to discuss issues longer just because everything is new.

The client's presence at the shoot is key for several reasons. First, the client must give his or her approval or request changes on the spot. Once a video is shot and everyone has disbanded, changes are almost impossible. Therefore, you must be prepared to watch what is shot very carefully and offer complete and specific feedback to the producer at once. Your comments may range from a question on pronunciation to a desk accessory that seems inappropriate. Your request may involve an addition to the script or only a change in an actor's expression. But it must be done immediately if it is to be done at all.

This is not to say that some changes cannot be made in the post-production period. But only the producer can tell you when that is the case, and you will have to trust his or her expertise on that point.

8 *Do the rough edit.* This is the first part of the editing process, the part in which the basic cutting and splicing is done. At this time, changes are relatively easy and inexpensive, so some producers will show the rough edit ("off-line" edit) to the client. However, this version will have none of the special effects such as music, titles, fades, and dissolves, so the client must not overreact to the roughness of this first product. The client should only be looking at what footage is included and in what order.

9 *Do the final edit.* This is called the "on-line" edit. It uses very expensive machinery, usually rented, and so must be done quickly. You as the client will be present at this edit only if there is a large number of technical additions, such as charts and graphs, and you must ensure their proper placement.

10 *Do the final screening.* If all has gone well, this is a festive occasion and a source of great satisfaction for everyone involved in the project.

How Can the Video Development Process Go Wrong?

If you follow the guidelines above, the development of your video will probably be a smooth, satisfying process. But you will want to be aware of some common pitfalls in the process, so that you can recognize and avoid them whenever possible. Such common pitfalls include the following:

1 *People try to put too much content in a video.* Video can present a few ideas very well, but if you have lots to cover, consider whether print wouldn't be better. Or use video just to get interest, then switch to print.

2 *One video is used to serve several audiences.* A typical example is to make one video, usually to save money, which can be shown to client, to salespeople, *and* to internal support staff. The objectives for each group are totally different; each group needs different information, which it will use differently. The result is a video that is good for no one.

3 *People try to cut costs unrealistically or in the wrong places.*
This may result in using amateur talent, taping in a real office,
leaving out important information, and so forth. These kinds of
cuts always affect the final product. Good video is expensive. If
the budget is not there, use a medium that is less expensive and
use it well. People often use parameters of $ per minute of
video. However, the justifiable cost per minute will vary wildly,
depending on the content and scenario. A per-minute price that
would be quite logical for one video might be outrageous for
another, even one on the same subject.

4 *Client and producer don't communicate enough.* This can be
because the client doesn't *know* what he or she really wants. Or
the client may be intimidated by the producer. Or the producer
may not take the time to ask questions and to probe. If there is
no ongoing dialogue between client and producer throughout
the project, the end result is often not what the client wanted.

5 *The client does not trust the producer.* As a result, the producer's
expertise in the video field is not used and, unless the client is
unusually knowledgeable, the result is amateurish.

6 *The proposal and budget are not clear and complete.* This may
result in misunderstandings about the process, the final results
wanted, or the costs.

7 *The scope expands without being monitored.* When the basic
objectives of the video change and no one recognizes the fact,
the original scenario may no longer apply. When this happens
the results are often disappointing.

PART

3

GLOSSARY
AND
INDEX

GLOSSARY

Back-home something that relates to or involves the learner's normal job environment, as in "back-home" planning or "back-home" problem.

Behavior modeling a learning methodology in which learners are given a step-by-step model for handling an interactive situation. They see someone using the model well, usually on video tape, then practice using the model themselves. Afterward they receive feedback on their practice.

Case study (also Case) a description of a situation in writing, on audio tape, or on video tape, which participants study and then discuss, guided by the questions and probing of an instructor.

Closed or close-ended questionnaire a questionnaire in which respondents choose their answers from the limited number of responses provided.

Closure a feeling of completeness or sense of accomplishment at the end of an activity.

Content analysis a process for analyzing subjective data to establish the major conclusions or themes that emerge.

Customize to adapt or create something to fit the specialized needs of a particular group of learners, as in a customized case or a customized program.

Design see Program design.

Design fit the degree to which certain materials carry out the intention of the program design; sometimes used to mean the degree to which a program's design fits the people for whom it was designed.

Design Document a written record of the points decided on in the design process, including content, process, objectives, and sequence of activities.

The Design Document guides the development of the program and any later modifications.

Design meeting a meeting in which the design of a training program is established.

Design team the group of people who actually attend the design meeting and make the decisions that establish the design of the program. The same people may also become involved in the program's development.

Development needs skills or knowledge that will be needed for a person's performance in a future position or at a later time.

Discovery learning a program participant's discovering a learning point through experiencing and analyzing a situation rather than through being told the learning point. Often used synonymously with experiential learning.

Experiential learning a program participant's learning through a classroom or outside experience rather than through being given information. Often used synonymously with discovery learning.

Facilitator a group or class leader whose main role is to guide and manage the learning process rather than to impart information.

Feedback information and reactions given to a person about his or her actions. Can be negative, positive, or a combination of the two.

Fishbowl a type of role-play in which a small number of participants perform the role-play in front of the rest of the class.

Flow see Program flow.

Game a formalized activity, usually unrelated to the business environment. The participants attempt to meet a defined objective within the limitations imposed by a set of rules, which determine the game's activities and termination.

Gateway a case used in the beginning of a unit or program to stimulate thinking about a topic or to introduce an exercise but often having no specific learning points of its own.

Group discussion planned opportunity for participants to freely exchange ideas, reactions, or opinions in a group setting under the direction of an instructor or group facilitator.

Individual exercise an exercise in which each participant works independently, usually to transfer the content or learning points of the program to his or her own situation.

Instructor the leader of a training program session. The instructor's role can range from giving all of the information to only guiding the learning process, depending on the design of the program.

Instructor notes a document outlining how the training program is to be conducted. Can range from a general outline to a word-for-word script.

Interactive involving action and discussion among learners or between learners and instructors. It also refers to something that involves interaction between two or more people, as in interactive situation or interactive exercise.

Interview guide a written document containing questions to be asked during an interview. May also include a suggested sequence and alternate paths of questioning.

Job aid an item designed to help the learner when he or she returns to the job, such as a manual, an audio or a video tape, a checklist, a model, or a planning form.

Learning methodology (also Learning method) the type of exercise or other activity used to help learning take place during a training program, such as an individual exercise, a role-play, a presentation, a task force exercise, or a case discussion.

Learning model the way in which learning takes place during a training program activity, such as an experiential model or a practice model.

Learning points the key messages learners take away from a program or part of a program.

Lecturette a short, structured presentation, usually used to introduce important new knowledge, topics, or activities.

Line review the periodic checking of program-related documents by line people for such points as accuracy, relevance to needs and objectives, or acceptability to the organization.

Materials see program materials.

Materials List a document that identifies all of the materials needed to conduct the training program. It is usually written by the project manager and is based on the Design Document.

Materials test a session in which the major program materials are tested in a classroom session with a group of people drawn from the future target audience. The test is not a complete session of the program, since only portions of the materials are tested.

Media   the means by which material is communicated in a training program. They normally include written, audio, and visual media.

Methodology   see Learning methodology.

Minicase (also Vignette)   a short case, which often asks participants to choose the course of action they would take in the situation described.

Modularized program   a training program that can be divided into parts, each of which can then be presented independently of the rest of the program.

Module   a part of a training program dealing with a clearly defined portion of the program content. Unlike the term "unit," module is often used to indicate a portion of the program that can be used independently of the rest of the program.

Needs Analysis (also Needs Assessment)   the process of gathering information about the people to be trained and their training or development needs. This information is then used to establish the content and process of the program. The term "Needs Analysis" is also used to refer to the information gathered and/or the document that presents that information.

Observer   during a training activity, a person who has the task of watching the activity and later sharing his or her observations and feedback about what happened.

Open-ended questionnaire (also Open questionnaire)   a written questionnaire composed primarily of questions for which there are many possible answers or interpretations. Respondents write in their responses.

Participant   a person who is attending a training seminar.

Participative   involving the learner taking an active part in the training process.

Physiological needs   the needs of program participants with regard to their physical comfort, concentration, varied physical activity, and energy level.

Planner   a workbook document designed to help participants capture the learning in a training program and/or to adapt that learning to his or her own work situation. Usually consists of questions or forms to which the participant adds his or her ideas, notes, or plans.

Pilot session (also Pilot program)   the first full presentation of a training program to members of the target population.

Presentation   see Lecturette.

Pre-work materials (also Pre-reading)   materials that direct participants to perform certain tasks required of them before they arrive at the training program.

Program   see Training program.

Program design   an outline or plan of what will happen in a training program, including program objectives, content, learning points, flow, activities, and timing.

Program development   the process of developing all of the materials necessary for the presentation of a training program. Sometimes used to include the design process; sometimes to include only the tasks performed after the design has been established.

Program flow   the way in which units and activities are arranged within a training program.

Program materials   all of the prepared papers, audio tapes, video tapes, or other teaching aids used during the presentation of a training program or in pre-work or follow-up activities.

Program Specifications Document   a document that defines the training or development needs a program will address, the people who will be trained, and any additional requirements or constraints the program must respect. It serves as the reference point for designing the program.

Program sponsor   see Sponsor.

Project manager   the person who is accountable for the design and development of a training program. The project manager may or may not be responsible for the Needs Analysis or the implementation of the program. He or she may actually perform the tasks necessary during design and development or may only supervise those who perform the tasks.

Project Plan   a document describing all the activities required to develop and test program materials, the people responsible for the activities, and the time frames involved. It is used to monitor and control the development process.

Project team   the group of people involved in the performance of design and development tasks for a given training program. Each person may be involved with all of the tasks or with only selected tasks.

Psychological needs   the needs of program participants with regard to issues such as confidentiality, interest, attention span, trust, and interest in learning.

Reality-test   an exercise in which participants, working in small groups, share their plans for action and receive reactions and suggestions from other group members.

Reviewer   a person who reviews program-related documents against whatever criteria are appropriate during that step of the design and development process.

Role-play exercise   an exercise in which participants simulate a real or hypothetical interactive situation. It is usually accompanied by analysis of what happened and feedback to participants about their behavior.

Round-robin role-play   an exercise in which there are several role-plays, so that each person has an opportunity to play each role at least once.

Seminar   an alternative term for a training program. It is commonly used to indicate a program that focuses on the presentation and discussion of information.

Simulation   an activity that duplicates a real-life situation, so that participants can experience and manipulate the situation and then analyze what happened.

Specifications   see Program Specifications Document.

Sponsor   the group or person who supports the development of a training program either financially, politically, conceptually, logistically, or through any combination of the above. The sponsor may also be the person or group who initially requested that the program be developed.

Subject matter experts   people who have specialized knowledge about a training program's target population and/or their jobs.

Target population   the people for whom a training program is intended.

Task force exercise   an exercise in which the participants, divided into small groups of three to eight, work concurrently on an assigned task or tasks, often presenting their results to the assembled class.

Technical review   the review of program materials by line people or subject matter experts to identify any technical or other inaccuracies. It does not include evaluation of the materials as training vehicles.

Training needs   the skills and knowledge the target population does not have but that are necessary for them to perform in their current jobs.

Training program   a scheduled meeting of people under the guidance of an instructor or facilitator for the purpose of acquiring or renewing skills or knowledge.

Unit   a part of a training program dealing with a clearly defined portion of the program content.

Vendor   in the training field, an organization that markets packaged training programs or services to other organizations.

Vignette   see Minicase.

Workshop   an alternate term for training program. It is commonly used to indicate a highly interactive or participative program that focuses on practical application of the content.

INDEX